Intensive Caring:
Practical Ways to Mentor Youth

Group
Loveland, Colorado

Intensive Caring: Practical Ways to Mentor Youth
Copyright © 1998 Group Publishing, Inc.

Credits
Contributing Authors: Rev. Harold Davis, Pamela J. Erwin, Steve Gardner, William D. Hendricks, Mark A. Holmen, Tony Martin, Mary Somerville, Barry St. Clair, Dr. Richard R. Wynn
Editor: Amy Simpson
Creative Development Editor: Dave Thornton
Chief Creative Officer: Joani Schultz
Copy Editor: Debbie Gowensmith
Art Director: Kari K. Monson
Cover Art Director: Jeff A. Storm
Computer Graphic Artist: Joyce Douglas
Cover Designer: Keith Rosenhagen
Cover Photographer: Tony Stone Images
Illustrator: Gary Templin
Production Manager: Gingar Kunkel

Unless otherwise noted, Scripture taken from the HOLY BIBLE, NEW INTERNATIONAL VERSION®. Copyright © 1973, 1978, 1984 by International Bible Society. Used by permission of Zondervan Publishing House. All rights reserved.

Library of Congress Cataloging-in-Publication Data
Intensive caring : practical ways to mentor youth.
     p. cm.
    Includes bibliographical references.
    ISBN 0-7644-2068-2
    1. Church group work with youth. 2. Mentoring in church work.
    BV4447.I497   1998
    259'.23--dc21
                                        98-17075
                                          CIP

10 9 8 7 6 5 4 3 2 1   07 06 05 04 03 02 01 00 99 98

Printed in the United States of America.

Contents

Foreword 5
William D. Hendricks

Chapter 1:
Helping Young People Become More Like Jesus 9
An Overview of Mentoring in Youth Ministry
Pamela J. Erwin

Chapter 2:
Equipping Teenagers to Do Ministry 31
Investing in the Spiritual Leaders of the Future
Barry St. Clair and Tony Martin

Chapter 3:
**From "We Shall Overcome"
to "We Shall Save Our Youth" 47**
Helping Young Men Make It to Adulthood
Rev. Harold Davis

Chapter 4:
Lenten Faith Mentoring 61
Using Mentoring in Confirmation
Mark A. Holmen

Chapter 5:
Women Supporting Young Women 75
Mentoring as Ministry to Teenage Mothers
Mary Somerville

Chapter 6:
A Modern Strategy Based on a First-Century Model 91
Mentoring as Leadership Training
Dr. Richard R. Wynn with Steve Gardner

Additional Resources for Mentoring 105

99099

By William D. Hendricks

Coauthor of As Iron Sharpens Iron: Building Character in a Mentoring Relationship

Foreword

When I was a boy, my siblings and friends and I were fond of whiling away summer afternoons at a public swimming pool down the street from where we lived. On our way to the pool, one topic inevitably came to dominate the conversation: the high diving board! (Those were the days before the fear of lawsuits had caused the removal of diving boards.)

"I'm going to do a one-and-a-half off the high diving board," my older brother would announce nonchalantly. Everyone's ears would perk up.

"You are not!" my sister and I would shoot back. But then we'd steal a glance at our brother's face, which beamed confidence. "Are you?" we'd ask, chastened by a growing sense of "What if?"

My brother would just smile his see-for-yourself smile and keep walking.

From there it was only a matter of time before someone else would chime in. "Well, I'm gonna do a handstand off the high dive!" my sister might assert, trying very hard to match our brother's bravado.

"Yeah, right!" he'd reply dismissively.

"You'll see!" she'd say with as much bluster as she could manage.

Another moment or two would pass. Then someone else would say, "Well I'm gonna do a full gainer! Off the high dive!"

And of course that would be met with a bevy of "No ways!"

As the youngest in the group, I usually listened to these vows in silence, filled with admiration and fear. Admiration because these brave divers were, after all, my family and my friends. And yet fear because if they were going to risk all for the honor of going off the high diving board, well then, of course I was going to have to go off the high diving board as well. And that would be a severe challenge! Would I be equal to the task?

What made this feat particularly difficult was that there was no way to assess the risks before you had committed yourself. Once you had climbed up the ten or twelve steps of the ladder and walked out on that narrow, bouncing board and looked out on a huge pool of bathers who you were sure all had their eyes fixed on you and looked down at that aqua surface a thousand miles below and at the drain at the bottom of the pool a thousand miles below that—well at that point you couldn't just say, "Oh, nice view. Think I'll try this some other time." Oh, no! Standing there on the high diving board, knees knocking and heart pounding, a speck suspended in the sky between heaven and earth, with six or eight other kids who were hanging off the ladder behind you and waiting and shouting, "C'mon! Hurry up!"—why, you had no choice but to jump! To take the plunge! To risk all! To throw yourself away in a mad leap, heart seized by a panic that lasted all of one and one-quarter seconds before dissolving in an explosion of sound and water and amazement that you were still alive.

I think about jumping off the high diving board when I think about mentoring. Mentoring is all the rage today. There are books about it. Conferences about it. Associations for it. Toll-free 1-800 numbers to call about it. And out of all this energy for mentoring have come the great stories of mentoring at its best.

For example, take Marva Collins of Chicago's Westside Preparatory School. Hers is a counterintuitive yet highly regarded model of mentoring: Elementary and middle school students in one of Chicago's inner city neighborhoods concentrate on the classics of Western literature—the Greek myths, the poetry of Chaucer, and the plays of William Shakespeare. Many magazines, newspapers, and TV shows—including Time magazine and *60 Minutes*—have lauded her accomplishments.

And in the Christian world there is Henrietta Mears. As director of Christian education at the First Presbyterian Church in Hollywood, Calif., she single-handedly re-engineered the concept of Sunday school, growing attendance from an already impressive four hundred children and young people to a seemingly impossible four thousand! Of those charges, more than four hundred went into vocational Christian work. One of her protégés was Bill Bright, founder of Campus Crusade for Christ. Another was Billy Graham, who said of her, "I doubt if any other woman outside my wife and mother has had such a marked influence [on my life]" ("Henrietta Mears: Dream Big," from www.intouch.org).

Stories like these are remarkably inspiring but also a bit daunting—especially if you don't exactly see yourself in a league with Marva Collins or Henrietta Mears. Sure, maybe if you had millions of dollars...or incredible conviction and determination...or visionary faith and the resources of a large, dominant church in a major denomination. Maybe then you could dive into mentoring at its best.

But as it is, you're just not there. You're on the front lines of working with young people where you can see the challenge at hand. And it's a severe challenge! So while you certainly affirm all the talk today about mentoring, you may feel a bit like I did listening to my siblings and friends talk about the high diving board. Nice to imagine—but perhaps beyond your capacity!

If that describes you, then I heartily commend *Intensive Caring: Practical Ways to Mentor Youth* as a shot of courage. This is the resource you've been waiting for—the one that shows how people just like you are learning to apply the principles and practices of mentoring in settings just like yours.

Make no mistake—the leaders profiled here are genuine champions. But they're champions you and I can relate to, offering models that make sense in the everyday church. You know the church I'm talking about. The one with limited budgets...hard-to-convince committees...even harder-to-recruit volunteers...and teens who (think they) have seen it all. It's in the crucible of real-world congregations like these that the examples presented in this manual have been tried and proven.

You'll find examples of weekly get-togethers lasting just one or two hours, ongoing clubs, phone mentoring, guided discussions, the use of drama and character role-play, even journaling. You'll learn how to use mentoring to establish new believers in the faith, ground communicants during the confirmation process, help young people develop skills in Bible study, and encourage them to reach out to their friends in evangelism.

You'll also examine the biblical basis for mentoring and look at models for both individual coaching and group mentoring. You'll learn that mentoring can be powerfully effective with both kids in trouble and kids who are becoming leaders. And where *Intensive Caring: Practical Ways to Mentor Youth* can't provide all the answers, it networks you to additional resources, experts, and organizations ready to provide additional help.

So I challenge you to wear out these pages! Study the ideas outlined here. Discuss them. Adapt them. Improve them. Add to them. But most of all, try them. Because I assure you that the future of a young person hangs in the balance! There is a young man or woman in your group who someday could look back and say that had it not been for you, he or she never would have become the person God intended. Knowing that, it is imperative that—like people presented in this book—you take the plunge!

So what are you waiting for? Come on in! The water's fine! And there's lots of company cheering you on as you, too, get into the action!

By Pamela J. Erwin

Coordinator of Youth and Family Ministries Program and Adjunct Professor at Denver Seminary in Denver, Colorado

Helping Young People Become More Like Jesus

An Overview of Mentoring in Youth Ministry

recently spoke with a young woman who is now a senior in college. I was her youth leader for three years, and we spent a lot of time together. She and I and another young woman met weekly during her senior year in high school. We studied Scripture together and talked about the young women's dreams for after high school. We had many significant conversations during that year.

As this young woman and I caught up on each other's lives, we both kept saying, "Do you remember when we did...?" or "Do you remember when this happened?" I was impressed by what she felt was important about our relationship. What she remembered, all these years later, were the ways I had showed her I cared about her.

Every year thousands of young people graduate from high school and go to college. For many of them who spent years involved in church youth groups, college is a time of moving away from their faith. The efforts of youth ministers and adult volunteers may seem to have been in vain. The talks and programs we thought were so good (and probably were!) may seem to have left no impact.

What young people do remember are the times we opened up our lives to them. They remember the adults who, through their actions and attitudes, told them that they mattered. Personal relationships are the key to nurturing young people into adults who reflect their full potential in Christ.

> *"We did this...in order to make ourselves a model for you to follow."*
>
> **—2 Thessalonians 3:9**

What Does Mentoring Mean?

Several years ago, I went skiing in North Carolina with a senior high group. Skiing in the South can be an interesting adventure; often it's more like ice skating downhill. And given my athletic ability, skiing is almost a suicide mission! On this trip, we decided to go night skiing because it had rained the day we were scheduled to ski. As you can imagine, since it had rained all morning, the man-made snow (only a couple of inches deep) was lying on a sheet of ice.

This particular ski area had only one chairlift, which took skiers to two runs: a beginner run and, higher up, a black diamond run. At the end of the evening, one of the other leaders, Vicki, and I decided to "make one more run," intending to get off the lift at the beginner run. As we approached the top of the beginner run, Vicki edged out of the chair slightly before we reached the jump-off point and crashed in a heap right at the bottom of our chair. Unable to get off without landing on Vicki, I cried out to the attendant to stop the chairlift because I wanted to get off. He stated that it wasn't possible. "What do I do?" I yelled.

"You have to go to the top!" was his response.

"But I can't ski!" The attendant just shook his head as I continued upward.

By this time, I was sweating and praying feverishly. As I approached the top, I got ready to exit the lift. As my skis touched the solid sheet of ice, they began a fast descent while the rest of my body headed the other direction. I later discovered that I suffered a slight concussion as my head hit the ice. Panicking, I knew I would never be able to get down the mountain. I didn't know that as soon as Vicki had reached the bottom of the hill, she had told the other adults what had happened. Everyone was nervous (my skiing ability was well-known).

Bill, the owner of the lodge where we were staying, was an excellent skier. He knew the slopes well at this ski resort. Bill quickly followed me up the lift. By the time he reached the top, I had gone only about one hundred yards. When he got to me, he said, "OK, here's what we're going to do. I'll ski down about ten to fifteen feet, and then you'll follow along in my tracks. I've been down this slope thousands of times, and I know exactly which way will be the best for you to go."

And that's exactly what we did. Although it seemed to take forever, it only took a few minutes. I may have fallen once or twice; I don't even remember. What I do remember is that thanks to Bill's knowledge and expertise, he was able to guide me safely down the mountain. He not only provided the tracks for me to follow, but he also gave me constant encouragement and advice.

That's what a mentor does. Someone who has been there before leads a novice through the experiences of life, providing the guidance and expertise to help her or him safely navigate.

There are two critical elements to any mentoring relationship. First, the mentor acts as a guide to the younger person, or protégé. The word "mentor" originated in Greek mythology. In Homer's *The Odyssey,* Mentor was entrusted with tutoring Odysseus' son, Telemachus, and providing guidance and instruction in the absence of his father.[1]

> *"You, however, know all about my teaching, my way of life, my purpose, faith, patience, love, endurance, persecutions, sufferings…Yet the Lord rescued me from all of them."*
>
> **—2 Timothy 3:10-11**

> *"Even though you have ten thousand guardians in Christ, you do not have many fathers, for in Christ Jesus I became your father through the gospel. Therefore I urge you to imitate me."*
>
> **—1 Corinthians 4:15-16**

The second element of a mentoring relationships is intimacy. A close, personal relationship provides the atmosphere in which a young person can watch the mentor's attitudes and actions, listen to what the mentor talks about, and learn skills for life.

Within the context of relationships, people can influence, impact, and change the attitudes and behaviors of others. Two factors make a close, personal relationship critical: modeling and imitation. Through words, attitudes, and actions, the mentor models Christlike values for the young person.

First and Second Timothy give us a glimpse of how Paul set this kind of example for his young protégé, Timothy. Paul reminded Timothy of the life he had exhibited and often reminded Timothy to let his life reflect the example Paul had set (1 Timothy 4:6; 2 Timothy 1:13; 2:2; 3:14-17). In the same way, mentors lead lives worth imitating and encourage young people to follow their example.

Mentors are beacons or image-bearers whom young people seek to imitate.

Because of the personal nature of the mentoring relationship, young people often imitate attitudes and behaviors without fully being aware of how well they're doing so. When my son, Shane, was in middle school and high school, he was active in our church's youth group. He spent a significant amount of time with one volunteer adult leader. Nelson was a counselor at most retreats and camps, and he was available whenever a young person needed advice or counsel. A couple of years ago, I remarked to Shane that he had developed into quite a "Southern gentleman." He smiled and said, "Thanks. I guess I always wanted to be like Nelson. I like the way he treats people." Shane had begun to imitate the behavior Nelson had modeled for him.

It's important to note, however, that young people will not imitate only positive behavior. Our society is full of young people who are becoming drug dealers, gang members, alcoholics, abusers, and white supremacists because of the negative behaviors and attitudes that have been modeled for them. Our desire is to surround young people with dynamic, loving role models to follow.

A mentor
- *is there,*
- *is a source of knowledge,*
- *listens,*
- *provides direction,*
- *helps identify dreams,*
- *is an advocate,*
- *encourages pursuit of dreams,*
- *provides correction,*
- *gives instruction and guidance, and*
- *is a wise and trusted friend.*

Why Add a Mentoring Program to Your Already Full Youth Program?

Jim and Anthony were an odd duo. Jim was a middle-aged white guy who lived in the suburbs. Anthony was a seventeen-year-old Chicano who lived in the city. Their love of music brought them together. They would spend hours in music stores, listening to the latest CDs. Jim, a product of the seventies, had a preference for rock music; Anthony was a fan of hip-hop and rap. Jim also played the drums and had begun teaching Anthony the basics.

Between their discussions about music, Jim had the opportunity to talk with Anthony about how he was doing in school, about what was going on with his family, and about his relationship with Jesus Christ. Anthony watched Jim be a father and a husband.

Years later, Anthony commented that Jim had greatly influenced the direction his life had taken. He had a desire to be the kind of man Jim was. Because relationships make a serious difference in a young person's life, mentoring is an important part of any youth ministry program. Here are three specific reasons mentoring relationships are important to teens:

1. Young people make better choices when adults mentor them.

Numerous studies have shown that young people who are involved in mentoring relationships with positive adult role models are far more likely to make positive life choices. For example, a recent study by Big Brothers Big Sisters of America showed that young people with mentors were far less likely to begin using illegal drugs or alcohol. This and other studies have shown that a teenager with a mentor will be
- more likely to stay in school,
- more likely to attend class,
- more likely to go to college,
- more hopeful about his or her future, and
- less likely to hit someone.[2]

2. Teenagers need close adult relationships.

In today's society, people are increasingly isolated from one-to-one human contact. With e-mail, voice mail, fax machines, and a variety of other electronic wizardry, we now can "interact" with people without actually talking to or seeing anyone. We have the ability to connect with our world through computers, the World Wide Web, and a seemingly infinite number of cable channels—all from the privacy of our own rooms.

A mentor is not
- *a parent,* • *a peer,*
- *a bank,* • *God, or*
  - *perfect.*

For teenagers, this lack of personal contact is particularly serious. Teenagers have far fewer caring adults involved in their lives than they used to. And during adolescence, young people are in desperate need of adults to encourage them as they develop emotionally, physically, and spiritually.

3. Teenagers need adults to help them develop lifelong faith relationships with Jesus Christ.

A few years ago, GROUP Magazine surveyed Christian college students to determine why they had remained faithful to Christ in the midst of opposing influences. The study was an attempt to determine how youth workers could address the phenomenon of teenagers who were active in youth groups but seemed to abandon their faith when they left home for college. These college students cited four major influences in their middle school and high school years that had strengthened them in their resolve to remain faithful: accountability; responsibility; youth leaders; and special events such as camps, missions trips, and retreats.[3]

Accountability and responsibility happen in the midst of strong relationships with peers and adults. Youth leaders who pour their lives into students create lasting impressions that are vital to the lifelong choices young people must make—living on far beyond flashy programs. I would hazard a guess that if the college students had been asked what it was about camps, missions trips, and retreats that had impacted their lives, the answer would have been the experience of sharing lives that often happens at a deeper level when we take kids out of their everyday surroundings and their comfort zones. What seems clear is that the intimate connection between young people and committed Christian adults provides impetus for sustained, growing faith.

What Are the Qualities of a Good Mentor?

Jenny, a fifteen-year-old young woman, had lived two houses down from Maggie for three years. Maggie, a seventy-two-year-old great-grandmother, had lived in the neighborhood for forty-five years. She had raised five children, but now she lived alone. Jenny and Maggie first began a relationship when Jenny's dog got out of her backyard and wandered over to Maggie's yard. Jenny and Maggie talked for a few minutes about the dog Maggie had when her children were younger.

From that point on, Maggie began to speak with Jenny when she was walking her dog. Jenny soon began to call Maggie occasionally to check on her. As time went on, they found they had interests in common. Maggie loved to cook and took new recipes to Jenny for her to taste. Jenny developed an interest in cooking, and the two began to trade recipes. Every holiday, Maggie made a craft item and gave it to Jenny—a bunny for Easter, an angel for Christmas. Maggie then showed Jenny how she had constructed the object, and they spent time together as Jenny made her own craft.

All the while, Maggie asked questions about Jenny's school, her friends, and her family. Maggie also told Jenny about her life. Although they didn't attend the same church, they were both Christians, and Maggie took time to share with Jenny about her faith and her relationship with Jesus.

Maggie and Jenny talked not only about Maggie's life, but also about Jenny's dreams and plans for the future. Maggie listened and encouraged Jenny as she made plans for college. After Jenny went to college, one of the first places she went when she came home for a visit was Maggie's house. She counted her relationship with Maggie as one of the most influential in her life.

Maggie provided for Jenny what most teens need from adults. Maggie was Jenny's champion, encouraging her to try new things; she was Jenny's counselor, helping her sort through life's issues; but most important, she let Jenny know she cared about her.

As I mentioned earlier, our society has grown increasingly isolated; we live in our own cocoons. Even in most homes, each person in the family has a bit of personal space and easily can draw away from other family members. Most young people attend large schools where it's difficult to find individualized attention from counselors and teachers. Very few children live in communities in which they're connected to a larger network of adults outside their nuclear families. And often the stresses on a nuclear family leave little time for focused attention on adolescents. Through mentoring relationships, we can begin to help reconnect young people to adults.

In the last few years, a number of studies have evaluated what kind of person makes the best mentor. What most studies have shown is that good mentors don't have one particular personality type; after all, young people also come in all personality types. There are, however, three factors to look for in finding mentors for young people.

1. Intergenerational connection

Young people need to be connected with adults of all ages. Maggie didn't think she had much in common with Jenny. Because of the age difference, Maggie felt uncomfortable and awkward with Jenny at first. Over time, Maggie learned that Jenny enjoyed spending time with her and was interested in the stories about her life. Jenny's connection to an older adult enriched her life as she learned about Maggie's personal history, her struggles and accomplishments, and how her relationship with Jesus had developed over the years.

2. Same-gender relationships

Besides the obvious ethical issues of mentoring someone of the opposite gender, young people desire to spend time with adults of the same gender. Developmentally, teens are in a period of discovering who they are. It's critical during this time for adolescents to be in relationships with adults who will help them find answers to the questions "What does it mean to be a woman?" and "What does it mean to be a man?"

3. Common interests or backgrounds

In any relationship, the more the people have in common, the more they have to build on. This doesn't mean we necessarily have to match mentors with young people from the same ethnic backgrounds or with similar personalities. What it does mean is that mentors and protégés need to have something in common. If they don't have similar backgrounds, a common interest will make their relationship stronger and the mentor will have a greater impact on the young person's life. For example, Jim and Anthony were from very different backgrounds, but they shared an interest in music. Maggie and Jenny, though generations apart, shared a love for cooking and crafts. Our job as youth workers is to help mentors and teens find common ground through the application process and training (see the applications on pages 28-30, and the "Initial Training" section on page 26).

What Can a Mentor Offer a Young Person?

Teenagers, like the rest of us, are seeking identity and safety. Adult mentors can help teenagers by providing relationships that are safe—relationships in which teenagers receive positive guidance and support as they work to figure out who they are. We can do this by caring for teenagers, confronting them, being a champion, being a coach, connecting them, and being a counselor.

Caring for teenagers

Many young people feel acutely as if they aren't important to anyone, including family, friends, and society in general. What teenagers need most from adults—plain and simple—is to know that adults care about them and about what happens to them. See the "Ways to Show Teenagers You Care" box below for a list of ideas to let young people know they matter.

Ways to Show Teenagers You Care

- Be yourself.
- Help them discover new things.
- Remember their birthdays.
- Look in their eyes when you talk to them.
- Listen to them.
- Laugh together.
- Tell them their feelings are OK.
- Be honest.
- Share with them strengths you admire.
- Give them choices when they ask your advice.
- Surprise them.
- Suggest better behaviors when they act out.
- Delight in their discoveries.
- Share their excitement.
- Mail a card or a letter to them.
- Call them to say hello.
- Give them space when they need it.
- Discuss their dreams and nightmares.
- Laugh at their jokes.
- Be relaxed.
- Answer their questions.
- Tell them how terrific they are.
- Create traditions with them, and keep them.
- Use your ears more than your mouth.
- Make yourself available.
- Find common interests.
- Apologize when you've done something wrong.
- Keep the promises you make.
- Thank them.
- Point out what you like about them.
- Catch them doing something right.
- Ask for their opinions.
- Have fun together.
- Tell them how much you like being with them.
- Let them solve most of their own problems.
- Be excited when you see them.
- Praise more; criticize less.
- Buy them small gifts (such as stuffed animals) that represent something you admire about them.
- Let them tell you how they feel.
- Admit it when you make a mistake.
- Tell them how proud you are of them.
- Believe in them.
- Be flexible.
- Delight in their uniqueness.
- Accept them as they are.
- Let them teach you.
- Daydream with them.
- Celebrate their firsts and lasts, such as the first day of school.
- Love them—no matter what.[4]

Confronting teenagers

One important way we can show young people we care about them is by confronting inappropriate behaviors and attitudes. Of course, this can be truly effective only after we've built relationships with the young people.

We can accomplish this by

- resisting the temptation to rescue them, allowing them to experience consequences;

● being gentle but addressing inappropriate actions or attitudes directly;

● allowing them to fail while continuing to support and love them; and

● helping them sort through our cultural values, encouraging them to be critical thinkers.

Being a champion

Today's teenagers have few adults who truly believe in them. Mentors can celebrate young people's victories whether they're small or large. Applaud teenagers' efforts (getting a driver's license, passing a geometry test, making a good choice, being a caring friend). Teenagers expect adults to notice when they fail or do something wrong. Surprise them by noticing when they do something right.

Being a coach

Like coaches, mentors can help teenagers find out what they're good at and build on their capabilities. Encourage teenagers to try new things such as playing musical instruments, singing in choirs or worship teams, learning new languages, or visiting natural history museums. Help teenagers find their passions.

Be willing to teach young people. Take advantage of the "teachable moments" you experience together. You may have opportunities to pass on valuable lessons—how to change the oil in a car, the importance of education, why God cares about everyone.

Connecting teenagers

Since teenagers generally have contact with a limited number of adults, mentors can offer teenagers connections that are crucial to moving into the adult world. Mentors can provide three basic and vital types of connections:

1. Connections in the business world

● Take teens to visit your workplace.

● Take them to visit your friends' workplaces.

● Introduce them to your associates and colleagues.

● If you have an idea of what jobs they might be interested in, take them to visit relevant places of work.

2. Connections to school resources

● Help guide teens through the process of deciding what to do after high school. School counselors are often intimidating to young people. And the choices of what to do after high school are sometimes overwhelming.

● Get to know the school counselor. Encourage teens to see this adult as an advocate and to visit him or her to seek out opportunities.

● Take them to visit nearby community, four-year, or technical colleges.

● Help them sort through financial-aid options.

3. A connection to Jesus Christ

The most important connection mentors can help teenagers make is to Jesus Christ. Be open and honest about your relationship with Jesus. Be willing to share struggles and discoveries. Work through a Bible study, or pray together.

Being a counselor

Most teenagers know few, if any, adults who are willing to sit and listen to them share what's important to them. One of the most important gifts a mentor can give a young person is the gift of listening. (See below for a list of "Ways to Improve Your Listening Skills.") Mentors can not only listen to teens, but can also provide guidance, assistance, and advice when it's appropriate.

Ways to Improve Your Listening Skills

● Listen with your ears and eyes. (Watch expression and body language.)
● Listen for emotions, not just words. (What does the voice convey?)
● Make regular eye contact.
● Communicate acceptance and understanding through positive body language. (Say you're listening through your facial expressions, and nod your head or smile to encourage when appropriate.)
● Repeat what you think the person has said. This will help you clarify what he or she is trying to say.
● Don't be quick to interrupt.
● Don't be quick to give advice.
● Relax.

A Biblical Model for Mentoring

The term "mentor" is not found in the Bible. The word "disciple," though, appears frequently (more than 160 times) in the Gospels and Acts. The Greek word for "disciple," *mathetes,* is used almost exclusively as a noun, seldom used to mean "to disciple."[7]

To Jesus' disciples, being a disciple meant being in a relationship with Jesus that called for unconditional commitment to Jesus—not merely a relationship in which Jesus imparted information to the disciples. The hallmarks of this discipleship relationship were following and obedience, as with Jesus' call to us today (Matthew 4:18-22; Luke 9:23; John 1:43; 14:23-24). This relationship is unique and distinct from a mentoring relationship. Jesus discipled the twelve, transforming them into his image just as he does when we enter into relationship with him. Our purpose in mentoring is to help others realize an increasing transformation into the image of Jesus (Luke 6:40; 2 Corinthians 3:18).

Matthew 23:8-12 clearly shows that the mentoring relationships we have with each other are different from the relationship Jesus had with his disciples:

"But you are not to be called 'Rabbi,' for you have only one Master and you are all brothers. And do not call anyone on earth 'father,' for you have one Father, and he is in heaven. Nor are you to be called 'teacher,' for you have one Teacher, the Christ. The greatest among you will be your servant. For whoever exalts himself will be humbled, and whoever humbles himself will be exalted."

Jesus is the master teacher. While some of us are teachers, pastors, and leaders, we are together "a fellowship of his students."[8] Jesus' relationship with his disciples (students) is not our model for mentoring relationships. In Jesus' relationship with his disciples, he drew them to himself. In mentoring relationships, we draw others to Christ.

Jesus calls us to mutual servanthood (Matthew 20:26-28). As Christians, we're called to love each other, look out for the best interests of each other, confront each other, and encourage each other (John 15:17; Philippians 2:1-4; 2 Timothy 4:2; Hebrews 3:13). As we submit to one another (Ephesians 5:21), we can assist each other in becoming more like Christ.

In his article "The Disappearing Disciple," Lawrence O. Richards suggests that the New Testament church is the model of discipleship for contemporary Christianity. He suggests that "we have to turn to the New Testament Epistles. There we have to search for the themes that will show us how to minister in the Christian faith-community...We are called to shape a community in which the goal of discipleship—that everyone who is fully trained be like our Teacher—be realized as every member experiences progressive transformation into the image of Jesus Christ."[9]

The New Testament shows us that the first-century Christians ministered and served one another in a community of faith (Acts 2:42-47; 4:32-35; Ephesians 4:1-6; Colossians 3:12-17). This community functioned to show others who God is, its members encouraging each other to be transformed.

This is the goal of mentoring: to encourage young people to grow in the image of Jesus Christ. With the New Testament church as our model, we see that a mentoring relationship is best when lived out in the context of community.

The Importance of Community

Many Christians define mentoring as a one-to-one relationship between an experienced believer and someone younger in the faith. The emphasis is on finding one person to maintain an in-depth, long-term personal relationship with the young believer. They reason that this type of relationship is necessary for young people to grow and develop emotionally, socially, morally, and spiritually. "Mentoring is a relational experience through which one person empowers another by sharing God-given resources."[10]

I agree that this kind of relationship is at the heart of mentoring. But I think successful mentoring goes one step further. The goals of mentoring are best accomplished within the boundaries of community. With a team of mentors, the mentoring experience for young people can be broadened and reinforced. Mentoring is ideally a long-term relationship, with one person as a guide or role model. But brief or short-term encounters can be significant as well.

The value of community is that instead of just one person living out positive examples and values, there are several. For example, Max L. Stackhouse suggests that seminary students are better prepared and educated for ministry when they are able to see the seminary faculty as a whole as a mentor and model.[11] In the same way, the mentoring experience is strengthened when the teenager sees the values and personal interest of the mentor lived out within a larger community of adults. These adults provide a collective example of what it means to grow into a Christlike adult.

A mentor may be sufficient to begin the process of initiating a young person into the ideals of a faith and value system. In other words, the mentor lives out his or her faith and values, allowing the young person to see what's important to the mentor. But young people will often test those beliefs and values. As they do, the mentoring community becomes an "internalized source of conviction and support."[13] A mentor may teach and show a student many things such as love, truthfulness, and trust, but it is within community that such things are tested and experienced as reality.

Ways to Establish a Mentoring Community

> *"If I am a young adult, no matter how inspiring and compelling my mentor's vision may be, I must experience the conviction that if I step out on this limb to take a road initially less traveled by, I will not finally be alone."*
>
> **—Sharon Daloz Parks**[12]

In 1 Corinthians 12:12-31, Paul discusses the Body of Christ. The church is to be a unified body that encourages, uplifts, and shows concern for its members. The local church is called to be the Body of Christ for each other. "We are called to shape a community marked by the growing commitment of every member to Christ and to others."[14]

Functioning as the Body of Christ, the church can provide the community mentoring necessary to develop strong, mature disciples of Jesus. Three specific ways to establish a mentoring community include peer mentoring, parent mentoring, and church-wide mentoring.

Peer mentoring

Peers have an incredible amount of influence on the decisions and choices young adults make. In fact, only parents have greater influence. It's essential, therefore, to create a youth group that provides positive reinforcement for good choices and encourages young people toward mature faith development. There are many options available to adults in youth ministry who want to develop peer mentoring. Here are three specific ministry strategies:

1. Safe community

The first goal of youth ministry should be to cultivate a safe community. Community-building focuses on creating an environment of acceptance. Most psychologists agree that one of humankind's most basic needs is the need to feel safe. Youth leaders should endeavor to create a safe place for all students through every activity and every word.

2. Student leadership

According to Ray Johnston, developing student leaders encourages "a deeper level of care and nurture" through training and involvement in ministry to others.[15] This deeper level of care and nurture often works to deepen the sense of community.

3. Small groups

Small groups provide an atmosphere in which students can question faith and values, build close relationships with peers and adult leaders, and learn responsibility. Small groups also furnish an opportunity for positive community and reinforcement.

Parent mentoring

Parents have the greatest impact on a young person's life—beyond even peers and youth workers. We often lose sight of that in coordinating youth ministries. It isn't enough to keep parents informed of activities or to contact them only when there's a problem. Parents need to be a focus of ministry. Granted, youth ministry demands are almost always greater than the resources, but by strengthening parents to act as mentors to their young people, we'll strengthen young people. Here are a few suggestions for strengthening parents:

● Distribute newsletters that include critical helps and information about parenting adolescents.

● Provide support and information for parents with young people in crisis.

● Provide support and information for parents in crisis.

● Develop relationships with parents.

● Ensure that avenues exist within your church community for parents to meet their own spiritual needs.

Church-wide mentoring

In many churches, youth programs and teenagers themselves have been segregated from other ministries of the church. Youth are often deprived of important in-depth contact with adults outside the youth program. As indicated earlier, young people need to be in contact with a variety of adult role models. Church-wide mentoring involves relationships on four levels.

1. Adult youth leaders

It's important that adult leaders in the youth program are involved in close, personal relationships with young people. Whenever possible, establish a ratio of one adult to five or six young people.

2. One-to-one mentoring relationships

One-to-one relationships are at the core of any community mentoring program. It's critical to our young people that we pair them with positive adult role models. The dynamics of your particular program and the availability of adult leadership may sometimes make it difficult or unwise to establish one-to-one relationships. Matching adults with two or three young people is also an option. This group mentoring can foster a sense of community among the young people. The elements of this type of program will be discussed in greater detail in the "Establishing a Formal Mentoring Program" section. (See page 23.)

3. The church at large

The church needs to realize and take seriously its responsibility to minister to the young people within its community. Pastoral staff should endeavor to educate adult church members regarding the need to provide love, support, and encouragement to young people.

4. Students in leadership

Encourage young people to become involved in leadership positions throughout the church. This is a good way for young people to grow and also to interact with adults. Try some of these ideas:

Small-group Bible studies—Encourage teenagers to participate in groups of five to eight students, sharing leadership with adults or possibly couples.

Job watching—Enlist adults to have young people spend time with them at work. Set this up for one day, or work with adults to schedule one or two days a year when young people can spend the day with them.

Worship and praise—Encourage musically gifted students to participate in a worship team, band, orchestra, or choir.

Drama—If your church has a drama team, involve teenagers.

Rites of passage—Develop a series of rites that enable teenagers to take on greater responsibility in church leadership as they mature.

Deciding on a Mentoring Program

Before you begin a mentoring program, you'll need to decide what your program will look like. There are a few factors to consider. First, start slowly. Begin by making your present program more mentor focused. Find ways to put teens in contact with adults within the parameters of your existing programs.

Second, solicit the advice and counsel of senior pastoral staff members, as well as other church leaders, before you decide on a program. By talking to other leaders first, you'll be able to gain others' perspectives and feelings toward a new program. You'll also be paving the way for support and encouragement once you initiate your mentoring program.

Third, be sure to consider the resources such as finances, facilities, and skilled leadership available to provide training for the specific program you choose.

Once you've gone through these steps, you're ready to begin. Mentoring programs may look different depending on the church or parachurch organization and the particular needs of the teenagers. In the following chapters, you'll find a variety of practical working models. These models can be adapted to fit your own particular needs and ministry characteristics.

Incorporating Mentoring Into Current Programs

Here are suggestions for incorporating mentoring into existing programs:

Phone mentoring

A simple way of connecting adults with young people is through a phone-contact program. An adult agrees to contact by phone two or three teenagers a week to see how they're doing. Senior adults may be the most willing to participate in this kind of ministry. Requirements and training are minimal.

Requirements
- Commit to calling teenagers on a weekly basis.
- Make a twelve-month commitment to call teenagers.
- Participate in a training session.
- Follow up with the leader of phone mentoring at least once a quarter.

Training
Training should include the following information:
- How to have a conversation with a young person (See pages 22 and 23.)
- Ways to improve listening skills (See page 17.)
- What young people are looking for in a mentor (See page 27.)

Volunteer youth workers

It's important to encourage the adult volunteers in our youth groups to be active in mentoring young people. It's important to include a wide range of adult volunteers, from college students to young and middle-aged married couples, to singles and senior adults. Also encourage adult volunteers to be intentional in seeking out young people at youth activities and meetings. At the beginning of the year, have each volunteer identify five to seven young people to intentionally build relationships with during the coming year. Here are ways for adult leaders to cultivate and nurture relationships with students:

- Make a five- to ten-minute call to each young person once a week.
- Take each student to lunch or breakfast once a quarter.
- Send each young person a card or a note on his or her birthday.
- Invite all the students to your house to cook and enjoy a meal together.

The advantages of a one-to-one mentoring relationship (or one-to-two or one-to-three) are often immeasurable. This type of relationship is at the core of any community mentoring program.

> *"We know that when children have mentors, their school attendance goes up, grades improve and they are less likely to turn to drugs or get pregnant...There is [also] a ripple effect in the family—when you help one child, everyone benefits."*
>
> **—Matilda Raffa Cuomo**[16]

How to Have a Conversation With a Teenager

- Talk about interests you have in common.
- Ask open-ended questions instead of simple yes-or-no questions. For example, ask, "Who are your closest friends?" "What is your favorite thing to do just for fun?" or "What do you think about that movie?"
- Listen to their responses to open-ended questions, and follow up with more questions. For example, ask, "Why is Bob your closest friend?" or "What is it you like about Bob?"
- Volunteer information about yourself—your likes, dislikes, and experiences—when appropriate.

- Allow them opportunities to ask you questions. Don't keep the conversation one-sided.
- Make eye-to-eye contact as you talk.
- Practice presenting a friendly face—not goofy, but natural and relaxed.
- Pay attention to what they say. Show that what they say is important.
- Respect boundaries. Allow them to signal when you can delve into personal matters.
- Don't chatter simply to avoid awkward pauses. Silences are OK.
- Be yourself. Don't try to use their language to fit in.

Establishing a Formal Mentoring Program

There are some serious issues to consider when pairing adults in one-to-one, one-to-two, or one-to-three relationships with teenagers. It's essential to screen the adults before any match is made. Remember that meetings and activities between mentors and teenagers are usually unsupervised. Therefore you must provide adequate matching, training, and support.

Guidelines and requirements

The needs and dynamics of your ministry will influence the guidelines and requirements you establish. In general, though, these should be appropriate:

Time commitment

It's usually best to ask for a one-year commitment. Because of the nature of mentoring relationships, it will take several months to establish a relationship based on trust. A one-year commitment gives the pair time to move to a deeper level of relationship, where greater impact in the teenager's life can happen.

I've been involved in a mentoring relationship with a young woman for two years. The first six months of our relationship were awkward for a variety of reasons. Now we're extremely close. Had we made a commitment for only three to six months, we never would have gotten beyond that uncomfortable stage.

How often to meet

Usually a time frame of one to three hours a week is best. Obviously this is a goal and can't always happen, but it takes time to foster a close, personal relationship. Infrequent or short meetings won't allow mentors and young people to accomplish the goals of the mentoring relationship.

What the meetings look like

The nature of the meetings will depend on the personalities and interests of the people involved. I know one mentoring pair that likes to go in-line skating together. Since I'm athletically impaired, that wouldn't work for me. The mentor and teenager should determine, to a large extent, what the meetings look like. At first they usually experience awkwardness until they begin to discover mutual interests. Page 24 offers suggestions for things mentors and teenagers can do together. The following chapters also recommend specific resources mentors can use to initiate important discussions with teenagers.

A Year's Worth of Mentoring: Fifty-Two Weeks of Ideas

1. Take a walk around a lake.
2. Talk about your very first job.
3. Go to the library together.
4. Explore the Internet together.
5. Go to a movie.
6. Get together with friends from work.
7. Go in-line skating (or skiing or biking).
8. Make dinner together.
9. Go bargain hunting.
10. Go to church together.
11. Go to a concert.
12. Talk about credit cards.
13. Talk about your first date.
14. Work on homework together.
15. Go grocery shopping.
16. Change the oil in your car (do it yourself or take it to a shop).
17. Talk about college.
18. Visit a local college.
19. Go for a hike.
20. Talk about ways to find a job.
21. Go holiday shopping.
22. Talk about relationships.
23. Go to a play together.
24. Take tours of friends' workplaces.
25. Make popcorn and rent a movie.
26. Do a pretend job interview.
27. Talk about what you're learning about God.
28. Talk about balancing a checkbook.
29. Celebrate your birthdays together.
30. Talk about personal values.
31. Visit a music store together.
32. Talk about balancing work and life.
33. Talk about the things you have learned when you've failed.
34. Talk about networking.
35. Research colleges or technical schools together.
36. Go out to dinner together.
37. Visit a sick friend together.
38. Talk about dying.
39. Invite his or her family over to dinner.
40. Visit a bookstore.
41. Talk about the future.
42. Talk about balancing a budget.
43. Talk about career options.
44. Talk about how you decided on the job you have.
45. Share funny stories about your childhood.
46. Go to a health club or gym together.
47. Work on a difficult puzzle together.
48. Share what you've learned about a particular Scripture.
49. Visit a museum.
50. Have a picnic in a park.
51. Work on job applications together.
52. Visit the zoo.[17]

Putting the program in place

Interviews—It's important that both mentors and teenagers go through an application and interview process (see the applications on pages 28-30). This will help you make good matches and identify any unrealistic expectations. The applications should be either completed ahead of time and discussed in a personal interview or completed during the interview process. Either way, you or someone from your ministry team should personally discuss the information in the application with each applicant.

Background checks—Next you must complete a background check of every mentor, checking his or her personal references and checking with the appropriate law-enforcement authorities for criminal history. Your local authorities can put you in touch with the appropriate agency for your particular state. There is usually a small fee charged for a criminal history check, but it's well worth the effort and cost to protect the teenagers involved in the mentoring program.

There are all kinds of private investigative agencies that do background checks, but every state has a government agency that will release the same information at a lower cost. The name of the agency and the department under which it operates will vary from state to state, but one of the following should work for you: Department of Public Safety, State Bureau of Investigation, Criminal Justice Information Center, Crime Information Center, State Police.

Remember that background checks aren't foolproof. For example, in my state background checks evaluate only criminal history within that state. Information from outside the state isn't easy to obtain. Each state is different, so be sure to find out what information is available to you, and take advantage of it.

Training—Each mentor will need to successfully complete an initial training process (discussed on page 26).

If at any point during these first three stages concerns or red flags appear, address them immediately. Obviously you shouldn't expect perfection, but you'll experience less difficulty in the mentoring relationships if you address issues up front. For example, many mentors may have unrealistic expectations about helping teenagers; they may want to "fix" the problems they encounter. If you're aware of these expectations up front and address them with the mentor, you'll help the mentor avoid problems and frustration in the relationship.

Matching mentors and teenagers—I encourage you to take the matching process very seriously. Use the information from the applications to help you in this process. Look for similar interests or other connections. I suggest that matches always be the same gender. Discuss possible matches with your ministry leaders, and pray specifically for God's guidance.

You or a member of your leadership team may want to be present at initial meetings between mentors and protégés. The presence of someone they both know will often reduce some of the awkwardness. Remove yourself as soon as possible, though, and allow them to begin to interact on their own.

Follow-up training and evaluation

It has been my experience that the programs that have the most successful matches have been the programs in which intentional follow-up with mentors and teenagers has taken place. I suggest offering a follow-up training session for mentors once a quarter.

During each session, do some retraining on a specific issue such as problem-solving. Also allow time for mentors to share successes and struggles. A benefit of this time is that it connects mentors. Mentors receive encouragement and support when they realize other mentors are facing similar issues. Mentors may also provide each other with invaluable wisdom.

Follow-up training should also include evaluation. Ask mentors how they think the relationships are going. What can they do better? What are they doing well? Encourage them to see strengths and weaknesses in the relationship.

Allow mentors to evaluate the ministry, too. Ask them how you can do your job better and what you can provide to help them in their ministry to teenagers. Be open to hear what they have to say.

It's wise to follow up with the teenagers as well. When you see the young people at meetings and activities, take the opportunity occasionally to ask them how the relationships are going. Call them once a month, or every two months, to ask them about their relationships. You may find that teenagers are more open about their mentors in a group of teenagers. Get them together once a quarter. Ask them to share what their mentors need to know to be better mentors. Provide some training for them, as well, on their responsibilities in the relationships—meeting with their mentors regularly, calling their mentors if they can't make the scheduled meetings, and trusting their mentors, for example.

Initial Training

As I mentioned, initial training is critical to the success of the mentor relationship. Usually, a two- to four-hour training session is sufficient. Here are some of the topics that should be covered:

1. Education about youth culture
2. Listening and communicating skills
   - Ways to improve listening skills (See page 17.)
   - How to have a conversation (See pages 22–23.)
3. Roles of mentors
   - What a mentor is (See page 11.)
   - What a mentor isn't (See page 12.)
   - What young people are looking for in mentors (See page 27.)
4. Cross-cultural dynamics (if applicable)
5. Problem-solving
6. What's appropriate in mentoring
   - Meeting times
   - Meeting places
   - Touch
   - Conversation topics

Establishing a mentoring program may seem like an overwhelming task in the beginning. Break it down into manageable pieces. First be sure to spend plenty of time planning and soliciting support. Second develop guidelines for your particular ministry, and then start recruiting adults. You even might want to recruit another adult leader to oversee the mentoring program. Then aim for a few mentoring matches (maybe four to six) initially. Grow your ministry gradually.

I think you'll be amazed at the eagerness of teenagers to participate in mentoring. Today's young people are starving for adult relationships. One of the greatest gifts we can offer them is a Christlike adult to care about them.

What Young People Are Looking for in a Mentor

- Someone to talk to.
- Someone to say, "You matter to me."
- Someone to challenge them to be their best.
- Someone who takes them seriously.
- Someone who doesn't judge them.
- Someone who respects them.
- Someone who accepts them.
- Someone who understands them.
- Someone to laugh with them.
- Someone to be serious with them.
- Someone who cares.

Endnotes

1. Homer, *The Odyssey* (Cambridge, MA: Harvard University Press, 1976), 53.
2. "About Mentoring," One to One: The National Mentoring Partnership, from the Web site at www.mentoring.org.
3. Diane Fischer and Mike Woodruff, "Why Kids Stay Committed to Christ," GROUP Magazine (September 1992), 23-26.
4. Jolene L. Roehlkepartain, "150 Ways to Show Kids You Care," from the Search Institute Web site at www.search-institute.org.
5. Julie Gorman, "Christian Formation," Christian Education Journal 10, no. 2 (1990), 66.
6. "Respect Young People," from the Search Institute Web site at www.search-institute.org.
7. Lawrence O. Richards, "The Disappearing Disciple," Evangelical Journal 10 (Spring 1992), 3.
8. Hans Kvalbein, "Go Therefore and Make Disciples...The Concept of Discipleship in the New Testament," Themelios (January/February 1988), 49.
9. Richards, "The Disappearing Disciple," 10-11.
10. Paul D. Stanley and J. Robert Clinton, *Connecting* (Colorado Springs, CO: NavPress, 1992), 12.
11. Max L. Stackhouse, "The Faculty as Mentor and Model," Theological Education (Autumn 1991), 67.
12. Sharon Daloz Parks, "Social Vision and Moral Courage: Mentoring a New Generation," Cross Currents (Fall 1990), 357.
13. Parks, "Social Vision and Moral Courage: Mentoring a New Generation," 357.
14. Richards, "The Disappearing Disciple," 10.
15. Ray Johnston, *Developing Student Leaders* (Grand Rapids, MI: Zondervan Publishing House, 1992), 25.
16. Carla Rohlfing, "Women Who Make a Difference," Family Circle (May 13, 1997), 19.
17. "A Year's Worth of Mentoring," One to One: The National Mentoring Partnership, from the Web site at www.mentoring.org.

Application to Be a Mentor

We appreciate your interest in becoming a mentor. Mentors are concerned adults who commit their time, skill, and creativity to help young people achieve their potential through consistent relationship. The information in this application will help us match you with a young person and will be kept confidential.

Date: _____

Name: _____

Ethnic Origin: (Please circle) African-American Hispanic Caucasian Asian Other _____

Street Address: _____

City: _____ **State:** _____ **Zip Code:** _____

Phone: (H) _____ (W) _____ **Pager:** _____

Marital Status:

❑ Married to First Spouse   ❑ Never Married   ❑ Divorced

❑ Divorced & Remarried   ❑ Separated   ❑ Widowed

❑ Widowed & Remarried

Spouse's Name (if applicable)**:** _____

Child(ren)'s name(s) and age(s) (if applicable)**:** _____

Occupation: _____ **Employer:** _____

Birth Date: _____ **Gender:** _____ **Age:** _____

Languages (other than English)**:** _____

Would you agree to have us check your name through federal and state criminal records of child abuse and

neglect proceedings? _____Yes _____No

Social Security Number: _____

Please list any special interests, skills or hobbies, or areas of expertise in which you feel you can be of help

to a teenager: _____

Please list examples of any prior volunteer experience: _____

Please circle words that describe your personality:

Spiritual	Sensitive	Quiet	Outgoing
Adventuresome	Happy	Shy	Talkative
Confident	Moody	Nervous	Friendly
Enthusiastic	Impatient	Impulsive	Serious
Good-natured	Assertive	Bold	Cheerful

Other: _____

List three people who can serve as character references for you.

Name: _____ **Address:** _____

City: _____ **State:** _____ **Zip:** _____

Phone: _____ **Relationship:** _____

Name: _____ **Address:** _____

City: _____ **State:** _____ **Zip:** _____

Phone: _____ **Relationship:** _____

Name: _____ **Address:** _____

City: _____ **State:** _____ **Zip:** _____

Phone: _____ **Relationship:** _____

Please list one work reference:

Name: _____ **Address:** _____

City: _____ **State:** _____ **Zip:** _____

Phone: _____ **Relationship:** _____

As a mentor, you would be asked to make the following commitments:
- Commit to working with at least one young person for at least one year with the possibility of continuing the relationship on a long-term basis.
- Commit to maintaining weekly contact with your teenager(s) and to meet face-to-face at least once a week for a period of one to three hours.
- Commit to completing mentor training before being matched with a teenager.
- Commit to regular supervision and evaluation.
- Commit to assisting your teenager in identifying and achieving academic, personal, and spiritual goals.
- Commit to basing your relationship on respect for the teenager and his or her family.

I certify that the information I have supplied is correct to the best of my knowledge. I grant permission to contact the references provided and to complete a background check.

Signature: _____ Date: _____

Application for a Mentor

Date: _____

Name: _____

Ethnic Origin: (Please circle)

African-American   Hispanic   Caucasian   Asian   Other

Street Address: _____

City: _____ **State:** _____ **Zip Code:** _____

Phone: (H) _____ (W) _____ **Pager:** _____

Parent(s)/Guardian(s) Name: _____

Parent Address if Different From Above: _____

_____

Date of Birth: _____ **Social Security Number:** _____ **Age:** _____

School Attending: _____ **Grade in School:** _____

What school or community activities do you participate in?

_____

What do you do for fun?

_____

Please circle words that describe your personality:

Spiritual	Sensitive	Quiet	Outgoing
Adventuresome	Happy	Shy	Talkative
Confident	Moody	Nervous	Friendly
Enthusiastic	Impatient	Impulsive	Serious
Good-natured	Assertive	Bold	Cheerful

Other: _____

Why are you interested in having a mentor?

By Barry St. Clair and Tony Martin

President and Resource Specialist at Reach Out Ministries in Norcross, Georgia

Equipping Teenagers to Do Ministry

Investing in the Spiritual Leaders of the Future

Life invested in life! Can anything bring greater rewards? Throughout Christian history, leaders have placed extraordinary time, effort, and prayer into the development of future spiritual leaders. From Paul and Timothy on, every generation has benefited from the care and nurture of one person pouring his or her life into another.

Churches have typically done a decent job of imparting information in classroom settings. Unfortunately, that's often as far as it goes. While we're not belittling the necessity of proper Christian education, students need more opportunities and challenges than the run-of-the-mill Christian education program offers. One of the ways to use a mentoring ministry is to help students develop their own leadership skills. Mentoring is not an end in itself; rather, it's a process, a means by which students can be equipped and empowered to develop dynamic lives and ministries that are uniquely theirs.

What Is Mentoring?

At Reach Out Ministries, we define mentoring as the process by which an older leader invests his or her life into a younger, emerging leader for the purpose of spiritual character and leadership development in an intensely relational fashion. This is a fairly generic definition, but we put a high premium on investing in those young, emerging leaders in the church. In our model, we invest extraordinary time in those students who show the potential—or at least have the initial "want to"—to be a leader in ministry. While our model of mentoring may apply to all kinds of young people, future spiritual leaders are our focus.

Your Personal Qualifications

Mentoring is rather trendy these days; it's gotten to be one of

> *Mentoring is not an end in itself; rather, it's a process, a means by which students can be equipped and empowered to develop dynamic lives and ministries that are uniquely theirs.*

We define mentoring as the process by which an older leader invests his or her life into a younger, emerging leader for the purpose of spiritual character and leadership development in an intensely relational fashion.

those ministry buzzwords people carelessly toss about. So let's get personal: Are you "qualified" to begin a mentoring ministry? Is this an investment you really want to make, or even need to make? Stated more succinctly, is God in it?

Steve Young, who has developed our intern program at Reach Out Ministries, lists some qualifying characteristics for those who might consider taking on the responsibility of the care and nurture of a protégé:

You have a clear vision for ministry.

Know where you're going so you can clearly articulate that vision to a teenager. The young person needs to know where he or she fits into the big picture. The purpose of mentoring, to us, is equipping and investing in young people to the extent that they're able to take on some of the responsibilities of ministry themselves.

You are willing to sacrifice time and resources.

The young person needs to spend quality time with you. He or she needs instructions and appropriate responsibilities. Your young person is there to learn, not just to kill time. Most ministry is caught rather than taught; if you're going to duplicate your ministry skills in someone else, obviously that person needs to spend time with you.

If we are indeed the Body of Christ and a priesthood of believers, we should equip our teenagers as ministers.

You are dedicated to the spiritual development of the young person.

You have the opportunity to build into the life of another person. Look at this process as a chance to mold and shape someone with years of ministry before him or her. We don't necessarily encourage youth leaders to treat every teenager as a vocational youth minister in waiting, but if we are indeed the Body of Christ and a priesthood of believers, we should equip our teenagers as ministers.

You are tough enough to ask the hard questions, to correct and rebuke the protégé when necessary.

Kids will make mistakes—get ready! You'll need to be tolerant; the goal is to build up, not to tear down. Think of the mistakes you made as you began to take on leadership in ministry. Hopefully someone was there to coach you along. You can offer that same support to a young person.

You have the gifts and abilities of an encourager, along with a great measure of patience.

Enough said.

You have a clear sense of direction, with the whole mentoring relationship planned out in detail.

For your own sake, you need to know what you want to accomplish before the first meeting. Remember, you're entering this with the intent of being a tool God can use to shape a life. Know where you're going!

An Overview...

It should be apparent that we're not talking about just another youth activity here. If you're planning a trip to the beach or a theme park, all you have to do is publicize, get your chaperones on board, collect money, load up the bus, and hit the road. As long as everyone stays safe and behaves appropriately, your event is a success. How hard can it be?

Mentoring is an entirely different issue. For one thing, you have to spend a lot of time in personal evaluation. Is this what you want to spend a sizable chunk of your week doing? Do the potential benefits outweigh the significant sacrifices you'll be making? And if you have a bunch of apathetic kids, what gives you the idea that you'll find candidates for such an involved endeavor?

We're not talking about just another youth activity here.

We've come to realize that kids aren't on hold until some magic age at which they can contribute to ministry.

What Is Involved

Keep your head up and your eyes wide open as you consider mentoring. From our vantage point, here's some of what you're getting yourself into:

Why we do it

"Equipping leaders to do the work of the ministry" is our bread and butter at Reach Out Ministries. We've come to realize that kids aren't on hold until some magic age at which they can contribute to ministry. We mentor to build leaders, not just to offer some souped-up discipling ministry.

Where it works best

We ground all we do in the local church. But mentoring isn't just another youth activity. In our approach, mentoring isn't for every student. It's for those kids who want to make a mark in leadership, both in the church and in their "marketplace." We suggest that mentoring sessions take place away from the church building—in homes, parks, or quiet restaurants.

What kind of time commitment

Can you say "extensive"? Think in terms of a couple of hours a week for each student you're immediately responsible for. That's "formal" time; add to that "informal" time—taking your protégé on an outreach visit, for example. Add to that the time you take personally to prepare to meet, and you can easily see that this might take five or more hours a week. (Don't panic. You don't have to do this all alone—nor should you.)

What type of relationship

If you're the key youth leader, the relationship you'll have with your young person will be quite different from the relationships you have with the rest of the kids in your group. You'll spend more time with your protégé than everyone else, and you'll develop a closer relationship with him or her. Frankly there's the potential for hurt feelings and accusations of "playing favorites." You'll be able to head some of that off as you begin the process and explain what you're trying to accomplish, but be realistic anyway.

Beginning the process

Use the following suggestions as intermediate steps to get the ball rolling.

Evaluate yourself carefully.

What specific gifts and abilities do you have that are worth investing in a teenager? God has uniquely gifted you, and you have a unique role in a student's life. What do you have that can make a real contribution in your protégé's life? Conversely, what issues need to be dealt with in your own life that might hinder the mentoring relationship?

> *God has uniquely gifted you, and you have a unique role in a student's life.*

Pray for protégés.

We're amazed at how many youth leaders get a good idea from a book or at a conference and just rush blindly into another "program." Mentoring isn't a process to enter lightly. Pray specifically and purposefully for students to mentor. Even in the most unlikely or unmotivated group, there's always a "remnant"—perhaps only one or two kids—who have a hunger for deeper and more meaningful relationships with both God and caring adults. Pray to that end. Call on others to pray for the same thing. Even announce to your group that you're praying for kids who are willing to enter this kind of relationship.

Design the relationship.

Develop a prototype of what a mentoring relationship should look like. Be sure to include a description of all the expectations, both for the mentor and for the young person.

Take the "farm team" approach.

Dave Ronne here at Reach Out calls this "intentional bumping into." Always keep your spiritual sensitivity tuned to full alert. Notice which kids seem to take on leadership responsibilities, even informally. Be aware of those students who seem to have a degree of spiritual savvy. Don't fall into the common trap of gravitating toward the most talented or popular or beautiful or gregarious. Listen for kids to express that hunger to go deeper. Don't neglect the other students, but look for that "something" that leads you to believe you've got a diamond in the rough. Consider yourself on a constant scouting expedition. Be intentional in your conversations. Casually mention the mentoring ministry, and see if their eyes light up.

> *Don't fall into the common trap of gravitating toward the most talented or popular or beautiful or gregarious.*

Drop the bomb.

During your farming, formally and informally talk about mentoring to the whole group. (That way no one should feel excluded; most of them aren't particularly impressed with your new scheme anyway.) When the right moment presents itself, talk to the students you've discovered. Say something like, "You know, I've been talking with all the students about mentoring. I'd really like you to seriously consider being a part of that ministry."

Make sure you're on the same page.

After you drop the bomb, if the student doesn't scream and run, you can begin explaining expectations. You've already put together a prototype of what you'd like the relationship to look like, so you can clearly articulate what's going to happen. Set up another appointment with the student to go into detail concerning expectations. Provide a written document that explains the relationship (just don't overwhelm the poor kid).

> *You're finite, and you must consider the intensity of the other elements of your ministry.*

Get on with it.

Set up meeting times, make sure all expectations are clear, and get started.

To Group or Not to Group

Can one person effectively mentor more than one other person? We'd contend that it's difficult to invest heavily in more than one student. You're finite, and you must consider the intensity of the other elements of your ministry.

If you want to go the mega-mentor route, fine. Don't say we didn't warn you. We feel that a much better—and more effective—strategy is to equip a group of adult volunteers to help develop the mentoring ministry.

Practical Benefits of an Adult Mentoring Team

Here are some of the basic benefits of developing a team of adults to participate in the ministry of mentoring to teenagers:

Increase effectiveness through delegation.

Delegation will expand your influence as you learn to let go. That influence can go places you could never go.

Eliminate a multitask environment.

As finite creatures, there are just a handful of things we're really good at. Why frustrate yourself and cripple the ministry by keeping your hand in things that can be better "farmed out" to others to allow you to concentrate in the areas of your gifting? If mentoring is your passion, devote time to that while equipping your other adult leaders to do the things you might not be particularly good at. And even more important, if you have a mentoring "team," the protégés can receive the one-to-one time and equipping we truly believe is essential to the success of a mentoring ministry.

Provide better pastoral care for students.

Can you really adequately, personally, and comprehensively minister to forty kids? Thirty? Twelve? As numbers grow, personal attention suffers. This is not a weakness; it's a reality. And it's possible that for some reason some of the kids in your community or church just don't like you. Does that mean your ministry can't (or shouldn't) reach out to them? With an effective team and practical application of the Body of Christ, there's no reason any student shouldn't be ministered to.

Allow others to share in the joys of ministry.

Youth ministry can bring intense personal satisfaction. Don't keep that to yourself. There's joy in watching the growth of young lives. Imagine the rare treat of having one of your adults experience the same reward you have!

Eliminate the loneliness of ministry.

We don't talk much about the isolation that comes in ministry. The plague of "no one understands" can afflict anyone. God made us social beings. He never intended for us to face life's struggles totally alone. God is always with us, but as a special treat he often manifests himself through the warmth and compassion of fellow human beings. Surrounded by those of similar vision, similar goals, and similar passions, youth leaders will find their confidence growing.

Build innovation for the entire ministry.

You may not feel all that clever or innovative. But all of us are smarter than one of us. Celebrate the differences and life experiences we all bring to the table.

Work in the areas of your strengths.

Do what you do best with excellence and all your heart. Don't fret over your areas of weakness. In the ministry of mentoring, kids can be matched with adults who have similar interests.

Complement your weaknesses.

Kids need to see that to lead and minister, they don't have to be superhuman. What better venue than mentoring for kids to see this reality lived out in your life and the lives of the other adults?

Keeping Your Leadership Team Motivated and on Task

You'll have to invest time in training and equipping those adults on your mentoring team. Here are some ideas for keeping and motivating adults:

Know where you're going.

People will invest themselves only if the leader's vision and plan are worthy of their investment. Be sure volunteers know your mission statement, your basic objectives, and your ministry distinctives before they take the job.

> *If you have a mentoring "team," the protégés can receive the one-to-one time and equipping we truly believe is essential to the success of a mentoring ministry.*

> *Youth ministry can bring intense personal satisfaction. Don't keep that to yourself.*

> *People will invest themselves only if the leader's vision and plan are worthy of their investment.*

Lead in character, vision, integrity, and purpose.

People are attracted to those who know where they're going and who will get there with integrity. Be personally committed to a cause that will outlive you and will encourage others to join you for the ride. Is mentoring your cause? Go for it!

Know what you're looking for in volunteers.

Better to have too little with the right people than too much with the wrong people. Have high standards that are specific and written.

Realize that not everyone fits into your strategy.

Invest time and funds in learning who the volunteers are and how they're uniquely motivated. Spiritual gift inventories, personality profiles, and work preference discoveries will save you enormous time, energy, and problems in the future. Be honest with a volunteer who in reality should be matched with another ministry expression. Most people appreciate honesty as the greatest sign of love for them personally.

Train every volunteer.

Training gives confidence. Confidence gives results. Remember the four stages of equipping: (1) I do it and they watch, (2) I do it and they do it with me, (3) they do it and I am with them, and (4) they do it and I am in the background to encourage.

Give volunteers meaningful responsibility.

Challenge volunteers to specific tasks with specific job descriptions. And be sure volunteers know the measurable criteria for completing the tasks in an excellent manner.

Communicate with each volunteer.

Let volunteers know specifically how their roles fit into the plan and how the ministry is changed by their contributions. People are motivated by the changes they sense coming from their involvement.

Provide consistent review and accountability.

Most volunteers will respond well if they receive honest evaluations with additional training.

Allow volunteers to fail.

Constantly communicate to your team that you give them permission to fail. Adults learn best by experience. The pain of an initial learning curve will yield great results down the road of time.

> *Not everyone fits into your strategy.*

> *People are motivated by the changes they sense coming from their involvement.*

Learn to live with the tension of working with people.

Problems are essential for progress. People are essential for progress. If you have people, you'll have problems.

Be a lover of people.

Understand that building volunteers will result in far more fruitfulness in ministry than doing the task yourself. Minister to people rather than recruit. Watch them ask to join your team.

Avoid those who sap your vision.

Volunteers will gravitate to your level of enthusiasm. Spend at least 10 percent of your day in quiet reflection and planning to keep yourself fresh.

Training Volunteers to Be Mentors

So when you've drafted your team and given volunteers an overview of the goals of the mentoring ministry, what do you do with them next?

Provide necessary materials.

We suggest that you use a book such as *Building Leaders for Strategic Youth Ministry* by Barry St. Clair. While *Building Leaders for Strategic Youth Ministry* wasn't written for the sole purpose of developing adult mentors, it does offer a "cookbook" approach to equipping adults for any aspect of youth ministry. Other resources include this book and those listed in the "Additional Resources for Mentoring" section on page 105.

Set up a training schedule.

We suggest four to six training sessions with volunteers. Use the previous section as a checklist for what you want to accomplish in your times together: Volunteers should understand the cause, the benefits of their involvement, and their own personal walk of faith.

Train.

The best way to train is to model, in workshop form, just exactly what each mentoring session should look like. This will answer the questions, "What do I do?" and "How do I do it?" The following section gives some ideas.

The Mentoring Tool Kit

While there are scores of ways to do mentoring, we'd like to offer one possible model. Remember that this is one model, not the definitive word. You might use this as a template to get started in developing your own ideas.

Step one: Determine the time investment necessary.

Plan to spend one-and-a-half to two hours in a typical mentoring session. It generally takes that long to settle in, handle small talk, and warm up to each other. Less time would shortchange you both; longer would be unreasonable.

You'll also want to plan time for "extracurricular" events. Much of the mentoring relationship happens outside the regular meeting time.

You also need to take into consideration whatever personal preparation time you might need on a weekly basis.

Step two: Determine the length of the relationship.

You'll probably want the relationship to last for a lifetime. But you need "hopping on" and "jumping off" points for the formal mentoring time. We suggest a thirty-session commitment. This covers weekly meetings over the course of a school year, from September to May, with weeks off for holidays and other events. It's unlikely that you can sustain a mentoring relationship in the summer.

Step three: Determine the content of the relationship.

Here's where the fun begins. In building a mentoring relationship with a student, you both have certain obligations and responsibilities to consider.

There should be an element of "customization" to the mentoring relationship. At the same time, we suggest that certain basics should be included in the ministry (these are adapted from suggestions from Steve Young):

Start your protégé on a reading program.

Recommend books that have impacted your own life and ministry. Read these books with your teenager, and then discuss them together. Don't swamp the student, but do challenge him or her. When selecting books, take into consideration the felt needs of the student.

Emphasize and give tools to enhance spiritual growth.

Teach or re-emphasize skills such as Scripture memory, inductive Bible study, prayer, journaling, and sharing faith with others.

Show your young person why you do certain things in ministry.

He or she needs to observe your own leadership methods and to know the reason behind the activities you plan. (Make sure every program and activity has a purpose!)

Give your teenager growing responsibility as he or she is ready for it.

Let the student take on leadership roles in youth ministry.

Have your young person do mundane jobs.

For example, the student can set up chairs or sweep out the bus. He or she needs to learn that ministry has its "un-fun" tasks. Your intent is to prepare the young person for future leadership and ministry; while that might not necessarily be vocational, you do want to equip in the spirit of Ephesians 4.

Constantly push your teenager to learn.

If he or she sees something unpleasant happen at church—a strained relationship,

> *You'll probably want the relationship to last for a lifetime. But you need "hopping on" and "jumping off" points for the formal mentoring time.*

> *Your protégé needs to learn that ministry has its "un-fun" tasks.*

for example—ask, "What did you learn from that?"

Step four: Recruit.

Here are some practical recruiting ideas:

Pray.

Ask the Lord to give you specific direction. Pray for wisdom about who should be involved in your first attempt at mentoring. We suggest that you "pilot" the ministry with one student for a few months and then equip other adults.

Dream.

What would happen if the students you and your team mentor took their faith as their own? Dream a little. How would your church be affected? campuses? your community? Imagine what could happen in the ministry when it's properly in line with God's direction!

Select.

Make sure the whole group knows about your mentoring plans. Don't make a big deal of it; just mention it frequently. Then contact those students who are ready to go on with God. Give them a face-to-face challenge. You will have given everyone an opportunity to respond, but also you will have chosen the students who seem most likely to respond.

You might also consider developing an application form that outlines what the relationship involves. In the event that you have exceptional response from kids wanting mentors, you can have information about them handy so they might be matched later with adults. See the application form on page 30.

You might have a student or an adult wanting to enter this kind of relationship and without a "match." Don't force a relationship. Better to wait than to make a mistake here! By the way, don't mix genders in mentoring relationships—women mentor girls, men mentor guys.

Commit.

The students need to understand the nature of the mentoring commitment. Time may be the biggest barrier for your students. Be up front about the time commitment involved. In reality, most kids—especially if they're involved in extracurricular activities—know what it's like to make a commitment, and they're also aware of the time any worthwhile commitment might take.

Step five: Meet.

So...what does the actual mentoring session look like? Here are some suggestions for your first two meetings together:

Meeting One

Discuss these questions:

● In your relationship with Christ, what events have helped contribute to who you are today?

● Who has made the single most significant spiritual impact in your life?

● Are there any special ways God has used you? How might God want to use you in the days ahead?

● What is one thing both of us would like to gain from this relationship?

Spend some time praying together.

Make some specific assignments for the next week, including devotional times, reading assignments, and journaling.

Meeting Two

Talk about expectations in the relationship that might have come up since last week. Make sure all the agreed-upon expectations are reasonable and realistic, yet challenging. Talk about commitments and accountability.

Share insights from journaling and quiet time.

Pray together.

Make next week's assignments.

Of course there are many other ways the mentoring relationship can begin. Look below for suggested discussion topics.

Step six: Evaluate.

Take time after each session to ponder these questions:

● Did we accomplish our session objectives?

● Are there any areas of progress worth noting?

● Have any problem issues arisen?

● Does the student seem to be involved and spirited?

● Does the student need encouragement or admonishment?

● Are we tracking toward our goals?

More practical suggestions

Topics for weekly discussions

As you develop your sessions, consider these topic ideas:

● Assurance of salvation
● Time alone with God
● Dealing with temptation
● Asking for forgiveness
● Relationships with other Christians
● Understanding the Bible
● Taking notes
● How to read the Bible
● Inductive Bible study
● Memorizing Scripture
● Elements of prayer
● Developing a personal testimony
● Relational evangelism
● Sharing faith
● Spiritual gifts

● Faith
● Understanding what love is
● Time management
● Stewardship
● Understanding discipleship
● Decision-making and the will of God
● Vision, values, and goals
● Obedience
● World vision
● Leadership skills
● Life skills
● Journaling
● Investing in others
● Lordship of Christ

Journaling

The purpose of having a young person keep a journal is to train him or her to live reflectively by contemplating what God is doing and might do. You might provide a three-ring binder to hold documents such as blank journal pages, a calendar, forms for keeping a prayer list, a reading list, and meeting notes.

The journaling experience should be fun. Encourage the teenager to capture thoughts before they slip away. Ideally the young person should make journal entries each morning and evening, considering these questions:

Morning

- What Scripture did I read this morning?
- What am I praying for God to do today?
- What character quality am I working on today?
- What goal am I working on today?

Evening

- What did I do today?
- What did I learn today?
- How did I see God at work today?
- What would I do differently if I could live today over again?

Reading assignments

Reading will teach young people to "feed themselves." While there are scores of resources out there and while choices in reading material will be based on the needs of particular students, here are books—some new and some classics—that will greatly enhance the mentoring experience:

- *Experiencing God* by Henry Blackaby and Claude King—This is a great resource and workbook to help young people know and do the will of God. It's available in a youth edition as well as an adult edition.

> *Encourage the teenager to capture thoughts before they slip away.*

- *My Utmost for His Highest* by Oswald Chambers—In its updated edition, we believe it's just the best devotional guide available for the serious Christian.
- *Basic Christianity* by John Stott—It's just what the title says.
- *Spiritual Leadership* by Oswald Sanders—This is a classic.
- *In the Shadow of the Almighty* by Elizabeth Elliot—What a great and humbling inspirational read!
- *Evangelism and the Sovereignty of God* by J. I. Packer—Here's motivation for the Great Commission.
- *The Lost Art of Disciplemaking* by Leroy Eims—This little book gives a great picture of what goes on in a discipling relationship and gives principles that can be adapted to a mentoring situation. Here's a bonus for you: The appendix gives a thirty-session set of training objectives for a disciple. With just a little tweaking, it easily can be adapted to your mentoring plans.
- *Transforming Leadership* by Leighton Ford—This is a gem. Leighton's ministry has inspired much of what we understand about mentoring.
- *Windows of the Soul* by Ken Gire—Seldom has a book been such a revelation. For

devotional reading, it sure is a fresh voice.

● *The Mind of Christ* by T. W. Hunt—Dr. Hunt causes you to aspire to having the very mind of Christ. Convicting and powerful.

Don't just simply go with our recommendations. Use your own resources, and think about what you've read that especially ministered to you and might have something meaningful to say to your protégé.

Ask your teenager these questions after he or she has read a chapter:

● What was the author trying to say?
● What was the author's main point?
● Do you have any clarifying questions about what the author meant?
● What ramifications does this have for you personally?
● Do you agree or disagree with what the author said?
● What effect will this have on your life, in the future or right now?

Time-management tools

We've been amazed at how many kids we've seen with personal planners. There are plenty of good organizers out there, including products from Day-Timer, Franklin Covey, and many other companies. Many of these organizers are available in student editions. These organizers can be used for everything your protégé needs: They can hold journal notes, quiet-time materials, prayer lists, and just about anything else. Group Publishing also produces an annual *Student Plan-It Calendar,* which includes devotions for spiritual growth.

Curriculum and other resources

While we don't look at mentoring as a classroom experience, you might find some sort of curriculum helpful—adapted to your needs, of course. We recommend that you become an expert in youth curriculum; besides the usual big names in publishing, there are several smaller, unheralded resources out there. Group Publishing, Youth Specialties, Navigators, Campus Crusade for Christ, Sonlife Ministries, Young Life, Youth for Christ, Fellowship of Christian Athletes, Gospel Light, the National Network of Youth Ministries—all these ministries (and others) have much to offer.

Here are a couple of good resources we recommend specifically:

● Reach Out Ministries—Reach Out offers a five-book, ten-session resource called the Moving Toward Maturity series. There's a leaders guide for the whole series. Reach Out Ministries also offers a book by Barry St. Clair called *Life Happens.* It's written to help teenagers deal with the big questions of life.

● Student Discipleship Ministries—Billy Beacham and company have put together some excellent topical student manuals. They have some spiffy student journal-type organizers available, too.

Essentials for Success

Strive for quality biblical content.

Fun and games are important, but kids can be entertained in plenty of places outside the church. If we try to compete with the world on the world's terms, we're going to lose every time. God's Word is the only foundation for life decisions and practical

> *If we try to compete with the world on the world's terms, we're going to lose every time.*

living. Where else can your students develop a relationship with God?

Build a sense of friendship and community.

Your student needs a sense of bonding and a place to belong. The mentor must foster an open environment and make sure the relationship is comfortable enough for the teenager to be authentic.

Offer authentic learning that allows the young person to discover truth on his or her own.

The session doesn't function best when the entire meeting time is consumed with content. Protégés must draw from their own experiences and those of others to see if God's truth really will work for them. Never tell students anything you can lead them to discover for themselves! Using personal stories as illustrations—even the bad ones, within the realm of prudence and taste—will encourage students to take ownership of their faith.

> *The progress of the young person should be measured by the life change evident from week to week.*

Strive for measurable progress.

Progress is the norm! The young person cannot be satisfied to walk away from the meeting with just good feelings. The progress of the young person should be measured by the life change evident from week to week. Understand that spiritual growth is a delicate process and can't be forced—but growth should happen.

The focus of the protégé may need to be changed from introspection to a Christlike world view that includes others. Over time if a teenager can't begin to make inroads into the culture of unchurched students, he or she is too inwardly focused. It happens all the time. Students who reach out to others and share their faith enrich their own faith and see that the power of Christ changes lives. The teenager eventually moves from receiving from a mentor to giving to a needy group of friends.

Barriers to Effective Mentoring

Substituting control for nurture

Many mentoring relationships deteriorate into an adult attempting to control the actions of a teenager. A young person is often verbally beaten up when he or she doesn't live up to the expectations of the adult. Such controlling doesn't produce kids who are internally Christlike, but rather students who are externally behaving to please adults. This is a typical problem; we often want immediate results, and sometimes we'll manipulate and berate kids in order to get the responses we want. Mentoring is not a quick-fix methodology.

Lack of affirmation

As adults, we sometimes have a hard time being patient. We want to see our students become like Christ right now. When we see them struggle, fail, and sin, we're tempted to be impatient. Don't be impatient! Understand that maturity takes time. Focus on the things your protégé does right. Intentionally develop an environment of encouragement and affirmation.

Lack of commitment

Need we say more? It isn't profitable to bring people "kicking and screaming" into a mentoring relationship. You can't mentor someone who has no interest in being mentored any more than you can teach a pig to sing; it wastes your time and annoys the pig. Let's raise the bar and dare those who are ready for a challenge to get serious about God.

One Last Word of Advice

Above all, pray without ceasing. Don't use God simply as a consultant. God is the driving force, the instiller of the vision, the beginning and end-all of your mentoring ministry. Don't limit God. Without God, your mentoring ministry may be well prepared, well thought out, and executed with excellence—and cold and lifeless.

By Rev. Harold Davis

Associate Minister at Canaan Baptist Church in Urbana, Illinois, and author of Talks My Father Never Had With Me *mentoring curriculum*

From "We Shall Overcome" to "We Shall Save Our Youth"

Helping Young Men Make It to Adulthood

Several years ago a member of my church asked me to go with him to court because he was too afraid and nervous to go alone. When we arrived at the courthouse, I immediately was struck by the number of defendants I knew, including many members from my church who I hadn't seen in a while. Shortly after this experience, I was given a copy of the suspension statistics from our local school system. I found that black males were being suspended at a rate five times higher than that of other young men. These and other rude awakenings have caused me to focus all my attention on the need for intervention in the lives of our young people, particularly inner city youth.

I believe that when future generations assess our culture, they will with twenty-twenty hindsight discover that we were guilty of allowing communication between men and boys to slip dangerously below acceptable levels.

As a parent and a youth worker, I'm surrounded by kids, and at times I forget that my experience is not the norm. An unacceptably high percentage of today's men don't interact with boys at all. When mature, empowered men neglect to spend time with the next generation of men, their society will soon disintegrate because of the loss of core values to sustain it. No society survives long when young men must learn the basic principles of that society without the instruction, influence, and guidance of mature men. Our nation is facing a crisis; many young men have no concept of the principles that have made our nation great. The struggles of past generations are being lost; most of our young people have no historical appreciation or perspective. This lack of understanding will doom them to repeat the mistakes of the past.

> *When future generations assess our culture, they will…discover that we were guilty of allowing communication between men and boys to slip dangerously below acceptable levels.*

The Role of the Church

My grandmother taught that if a young man was to be successful in life, he needed to go to church. Recent research has confirmed her wisdom. For example, a study by Harvard economist Richard Freeman found that among black urban youth, church attendance was the best predictor of who would escape drugs and other destructive forces.[1] The problem with many urban young people is that they have no connection with God, so they do what is right in their own eyes. The solution as I see it is to develop a system whereby we can creatively connect boys with men from local urban churches. This must be done in a way that doesn't frighten the boys away or overtax the men.

The Bible is full of admonitions and commands for the church to address the needs of young people. As the father of four children, I'm committed to their welfare. But when I see the term "father" used in the Bible, I see a broader implication than just biology. I see God calling the spiritual men of our society to be fathers to those who have no fathers in their homes.

In Scripture, God warns of the negative consequences of ignoring disadvantaged young people. In Isaiah 1:23, God described some characteristics of Israel's fallen society: "Your rulers are rebels, companions of thieves; they all love bribes and chase after gifts. They do not defend the cause of the fatherless; the widow's case does not come before them."

I see this Scripture as a negative mandate from God, telling us that if we don't intervene in the lives of needy people, we'll find ourselves in the same situation. We can find many of the same characteristics in the modern United States that are described in the first chapter of Isaiah. At that time, God required the people to refocus on him and allow him to solve their problems (verse 18). This is the only solution for our desperate situation.

I also see in Scripture a positive mandate that should encourage any man to get involved in the lives of young people. In Job 29:1-12, Job was in an hour of doom and distress. In dialogue with his friends, he began to reflect on his life, highlighting the manner in which he had been esteemed by those around him. It's very impressive to see how God had elevated Job among his peers. His life had been full of social esteem, family, material wealth, and the blessings of God. In verse 12, Job revealed why he had been blessed: "Because I rescued the poor who cried for help, and the fatherless who had none to assist him."

God has a blessing in store for anyone who helps young people who have no advocates! Look at Isaiah 1:17, 19: "Learn to do right! Seek justice, encourage the oppressed. Defend the cause of the fatherless, plead the case of the widow...If you are willing and obedient, you will eat the best from the land."

It's a terrible thing to live in the United States of America yet to have no advocate.

> *Among black urban youth, church attendance was the best predictor of who would escape drugs and other destructive forces.*

> *"They do not defend the cause of the fatherless; the widow's case does not come before them."*
>
> **—Isaiah 1:23**

As I go into our school systems and observe young people in trouble, I see that those without advocates move swiftly through the system and toward incarceration. God is very concerned with the helpless in our society. The Bible says a lot about justice. "If anyone has material possessions and sees his brother in need but has no pity on him, how can the love of God be in him?" (1 John 3:17).

It's a terrible thing to live in the United States of America yet to have no advocate.

James 1:27 says, "Religion that God our Father accepts as pure and faultless is this: to look after orphans and widows in their distress and to keep oneself from being polluted by the world." When I read this verse recently with young people in mind, I saw something I never had seen before. The Scripture states that we are to look after orphans (the King James Version calls them "the fatherless") in their distress. This is a call not just to religion in general, but to putting our faith into action by looking after fatherless young people!

The Talks Concept

God has gifted me with an ability to communicate with young people. As an adult, I am very much in touch with my childhood. I am able to empathize with children, or feel what they feel. When I look into the eyes of a child, the child inside me challenges the man I now am to do something to make a difference.

My contribution to the solution has been to provide a tool that any man can use to impact the lives of boys. This tool is a mentoring curriculum called *Talks My Father Never Had With Me: Helping the Young Male Make It to Adulthood.* The book is intended to reproduce the kind of wise advice a father might give to his son.

I currently am working with my wife on a companion book for girls, but I chose to focus on boys as my first priority because statistics show that fatherless young men are the largest at-risk group today. I live in a largely middle class college town in Illinois. In one recent year in our school district, 239 students were suspended for disruptive behavior. Of these, 177 were males and 62 were females; 190 were black and 35 were white. During this same year, 409 students were suspended for physical confrontation with another student. Of these students, 282 were males and 127 were females; 312 were black and 75 were white. In all the other categories of suspensions, the numbers were about the same. These statistics from an average suburban school system validate my priorities, at least in my community: black boys, white boys, and then black girls.

The Talks curriculum is structured to help mentors address topics that are often hard to discuss otherwise. It creates the opportunity for older men to share wisdom regarding positive, ethical, and responsible living. It provides opportunities for constructive dialogue between generations.

Talks My Father Never Had With Me is available from KJAC Publishing, P.O. Box 111, Champaign, Illinois, 61824. This resource is available in three different editions: a black church edition, a public middle school or high school edition, and a public elementary school edition. A mentor's guide is also available for each edition.

How Mentoring Works

In this model of mentoring, the average session should last thirty-five to forty-five minutes. This means mentors can budget an hour to an hour and a half per week for the lesson, preparation, and travel time.

The mentoring group discusses one chapter of the book each week. The curriculum is used to facilitate conversation, teach values, and instill sound principles. Initially the goal is to expose the young men to mature men who can model responsible behavior for them and mentor them. Ultimately the goal is to lead the young men to make personal commitments to Jesus Christ.

Mentoring can happen in a variety of settings: in church, in school, or at home; in large groups or in small ones. I believe the ideal setting is a group of one mentor and three protégés in a local church. However, the mentoring model can be effective for fathers mentoring their sons, mothers mentoring their sons, long-distance mentoring (particularly by relatives), public schools, and the church.

Although mentoring is a creative method of evangelism and discipleship for unchurched young men, churches most often begin with the boys within their congregations. Each individual church must consider the needs of the church and the community and settle the question of which boys to start with. Remember, the goal is twofold: to reach out to those who have no other help or hope and to strengthen boys who are already in the church.

> *Although mentoring is a creative method of evangelism and discipleship for unchurched young men, churches most often begin with the boys within their congregations.*

Specific Features of the Model

The one-to-three approach

I believe the ideal setting for mentoring is a small group of one man and three boys. This approach protects both the man and the boys in several ways.

1. It reduces manipulation.

Men who aren't trained educators, psychologists, or seasoned parents are often easily manipulated by streetwise boys. When three boys are sitting around the table, it's more difficult for one boy to get away with manipulation.

2. It reduces the daddy-replacement syndrome.

Most men are "maxed out" already with family, job, and other responsibilities. When a man and a boy spend time together, that boy may latch on and develop unrealistic expectations of the man. This can frighten men and cause them to shy away from the mentoring effort. When a mentor meets with three boys, no one boy can expect the mentor to become his daddy. The boys look around the table and see that the mentor can't be everyone's daddy, so they generally don't develop those expectations.

> *When three boys are sitting around the table, it's more difficult for one boy to get away with manipulation.*

3. It reduces unhealthy dependence.

There is a danger of a boy expecting the mentor to meet all his social, emotional, financial, and even spiritual needs. Fear of unhealthy dependence can drive men from mentoring efforts. The chance of this happening is diminished when a man mentors more than one boy.

4. It reduces the chance of false accusations against the mentor.

It's a sad fact that mentoring does involve risk. Unfortunately, any time an adult meets privately with young people, there is a chance that the adult will be accused of abuse. This risk is minimized when more than one young person is present.

5. It increases the chance of a positive outcome.

Three boys offer three chances for success. Of the three boys in my current mentoring group, one loves the ground I walk on, another can take me or leave me, and the third acts like he hates my guts. What if I had been assigned only one? My experience would have been miserable if I had to mentor only the one who hates my guts. As it now stands, my mentoring efforts have been successful. I can see at a glance that two of my three boys gladly receive what I share with them.

Ministry to the mentor

All mentoring efforts speak of the need for boys to be mentored, but few address the needs of the mentor. I've learned that we will never have enough men to mentor unless we begin to address the men's problems, too.

Each mentoring situation involves benefits for the mentor as well as for the boys. Many men are dealing with unresolved issues from childhood and the disappointments of adulthood. Men are really impacted when they talk to boys who think the way the mentors thought when they were young. Mentors learn new principles or are reminded of principles they had forgotten. So mentors receive blessings and lessons of their own as they share with boys.

When men are transparent with boys as they interact around solid principles, the knife cuts both ways. I know this to be true in my own life and in the lives of many men who have mentored boys. I've heard many wonderful testimonies from men who were forced to deal with issues they had suppressed for years because the issues were brought up as they taught the boys.

Engaging Caring Men in the Battle

Men with problems in their past often want to help the next generation avoid making the same mistakes. With this in mind, you shouldn't automatically strike former drug addicts or inmates from your list of possible mentors.

We must learn how to prepare and engage men with problems in their past because it's becoming increasingly difficult to draw from a large pool of caring, capable men. (There still are caring, capable men, but many of them are already engaged in the battle.) In order to engage a man who is caring but perhaps not as capable, do the following things:

You shouldn't automatically strike former drug addicts or inmates from your list of possible mentors.

Enlist him.

We must enlist men from churches and communities. This must be an ongoing effort because many don't see the need immediately.

Disciple him.

Mentors must be discipled, regardless of age or spiritual maturity. Without wise counsel and ongoing input from other mentors, men can get bogged down and discouraged. They also can make mistakes that will render their efforts ineffective.

Educate him.

To educate the mentor is to show him the pain our young people are experiencing. When men see this, they're more likely to engage in the battle. Awaken them to the needs, and then show them clearly how they can help. An educated man has no reason not to take action.

The education process goes a step further when I show the man what he actually would do if he were to mentor three boys. I lay out the requirements of preparation, time commitment, and travel time in a matter of minutes so he can make an educated decision.

Encourage him.

If mentors aren't encouraged, they'll struggle to keep going. When you begin a mentoring effort, the enemy will double his efforts to stop you. Most men aren't prepared for this attack. I've seen this happen in church after church. To begin a mentoring effort without prayer support and other forms of encouragement is to ask for failure. For some practical suggestions for encouraging mentors, see "Encouraging Mentors" on page 55.

How to Set Up a Mentoring Ministry

I always encourage people to not wait for someone else to organize a mentoring ministry. I tell them, "If no one is available to implement this ministry, then it's obvious the Lord wants you to do it!" Here are some practical suggestions on how to start a mentoring ministry and keep it going.

Starting out

Step one: Appoint a coordinator.

In a small church, the coordinator may be the pastor, the youth pastor, or even a mentor. The coordinator is responsible for matching mentors with protégés, making arrangements with school boards if necessary, and generally overseeing the practical details of the mentoring program. In a large program, there may be one or more site coordinators under the project coordinator. Site coordinators oversee mentors in a given area, such as in one school.

Step two: Recruit mentors.

The coordinator's first job is to recruit mentors. I don't recommend advertising for mentors; the best way to recruit is through personal references. The main things I look for are consistency, trustworthiness, and morality.

Even if you know the prospective mentors, ask them to fill out an application. If the mentoring program is to be conducted through local schools, ask the school district for a volunteer application. Some schools also insist on a background check for the mentors. Generally if this is a requirement, the school will have a system whereby it can be done.

After the mentors have been recruited, the coordinator should schedule a meeting to give them some basic training. I've found that a session of about one hour is enough. The main purpose of the training is to give men insight into how boys think, characteristics of the age group they'll be working with, basic do's and don'ts, school rules and regulations, and some troubleshooting techniques.

If it seems impossible to equip men in such a short amount of time, please remember that what we're primarily doing is putting men in touch with their own childhoods! That's the most important tool for a mentor: the ability to empathize with the boys. If a mentor has particular concerns or needs for training beyond that, the coordinator can meet with him privately.

Step three: Identify the protégés.

Generally this isn't difficult because of the abundance of boys needing assistance! To form each group, or mentoring cell, choose three boys of similar age who live close to each other. Try to break up cliques and put brothers in different mentoring cells.

Be sure to get permission from the boys' parents to enroll them in the mentoring program. In some situations this may require a home visit, but it's worth the extra effort. Generally it's best to not interact with the boys without permission from their parents.

Step four: Introduce the mentors and protégés to each other.

If there is one mentoring cell, the mentor and boys can meet at a fast-food restaurant with the coordinator and establish the cell there. If you have a large group of boys, I recommend a dinner on a Friday night as the backdrop for the meeting. The first meeting for a school-based program will probably be at the school. At this meeting, the coordinator should give an overview of the mentoring effort and answer any questions. Invite the mentors, protégés, and parents.

Step five: Have mentors and protégés sign contracts.

One major component and teaching tool of the curriculum is the contract, which spells out the terms of the relationship. In the contracts, the mentors and the protégés are held to the same standards. Both parties promise to participate with good intentions, read, answer questions, and maintain privacy when necessary. The contracts also give the young men permission to disagree with their mentors! Have all the mentors and protégés sign these contracts at their first meeting. The duration of the contracts is usually one school year, but they can be adapted to fit the needs of individual situations.

You may want to keep the contracts handy during the mentoring process and review them frequently to remind the boys and the mentors what they agreed to do. I've found this to be extremely helpful, especially with younger boys.

Step six: Set up regular meeting times.

Establish a regular meeting time. In the schools, this time is usually during the school day, perhaps during a study hall period. In the church, this time is usually after school or on weekends. In some situations, a man from the church goes to the local school to mentor boys from his church. This works well because it puts church men in the lives of the boys during the week.

If the mentoring is to take place during working hours, the coordinator may need to help the mentors make arrangements to be gone from work. The time commitment is only sixty to ninety minutes per week, including travel time. I've found that employers are often more than willing to share one employee hour per week for such a valuable service to the community.

Teaching Tips for Mentors

Mentors—especially first-time mentors—sometimes feel nervous or inadequate when it comes to discussing serious issues with boys. They don't need to be educators, have college degrees, or even be good talkers; they need only to be willing to share with the boys stories about their past and the lessons they've learned. Here are more suggestions to help mentors:

Remember that you are impressive!

One of the points I like to stress is that most men have forgotten how impressive they are to boys. Young boys are impressed by our cars, our credit cards, our clothes, our wives, our ability to leave the 'hood, and many other factors. I suggest that we take advantage of this impressionability to reach them. When I drove to the 'hood to pick up one of my boys, I would pick him up in my old 1983 Mercedes. The boy would walk to the car very proudly because all his homies were watching him. Once in the car, he would adjust the seats to a cool position, and we would ride off. As a mentor, I used every advantage I could!

Drive time is a service and an opportunity.

When mentoring through a church ministry, the mentor should pick up the boys at their homes and take them to a neutral location. There are several reasons for this. In many cases, parents will not bring the boys, and the boys can't get to the designated location by themselves. Picking up the boys is part of your service to them.

The drive time also serves as a teaching time and offers some other important opportunities. The mentor must enter the boy's neighborhood, which gives him some perspective on where the boy is coming from. The boy is also impressed when the mentor comes to his home. I found that when I picked up the boys in my group, I had already impressed them!

Don't drag them into church.

If you're working with unchurched young men, don't take them to the church building right away. I recommend meeting at a neutral location such as a library, a youth center, or some other public area where you can have privacy to discuss the book. Boys generally expect Christians to drag them into church. Bring them gradually into the church building. I suggest quarterly informal spaghetti dinners where men from the church talk to the boys as a group.

Let the book be the villain.

The Talks curriculum is an off-with-the-gloves approach to mentoring. In other words, it doesn't beat around the bush or dance around sensitive issues! For the most part, boys know more than we think they know, and they can handle more than we think they can handle. Each chapter in the book hits home by addressing topics that are pertinent to the daily lives of young men; topics that would be difficult to discuss with a young man unless you knew him well.

I tell the mentors to let the book be the villain when interacting with the boys. The book presents the material; the boys can agree or argue with the principles in the book. The mentor also can add his own opinion.

Get help from the mentor's guide.

The textbook and the mentor's guide have been designed to take away fears of inadequacy and to encourage the mentor to enjoy the mentoring effort. The guide provides a one-page reading to prepare the mentor for each session. This introduction connects the man with his past and encourages him to let his experiences be an open book for the boys to read.

Don't rush!

As a mentor, never rush through a lesson; take your time. Each lesson will be different, and each will hit home with a different person. When you come upon a sensitive area, don't rush to conclude. Take your time, and let God work.

Encouraging Mentors

Even the best and most motivated mentors can become discouraged. Keeping mentors focused, energized, and encouraged is vital to the success of a mentoring ministry. I believe that for the leader to fail to provide this additional support is equivalent to neglect! Use these ideas to encourage mentors.

Each lesson will be different, and each will hit home with a different person.

How do I know it's working?

Because the benefits of mentoring sometimes aren't obvious for

Keeping mentors focused, energized, and encouraged is vital to the success of a mentoring ministry.

years, it's easy to wonder whether a mentoring effort is really working. There are several short-term benefits that will tell you the program is working:

- Men and boys can dialogue freely.
- Men are regularly spending time on a weekly basis with boys.
- Boys can repeat any of the principles shared with them.
- In public school mentoring programs, men from the community have become familiar with the school environment.
- In church mentoring programs, unchurched boys have an accurate understanding of what a church is.

The long-term benefits are even better. A strong mentoring program can contribute to racial reconciliation, generational reconciliation, and social class reconciliation. Each community offers problems to be overcome. Mentoring will help break down walls and barriers and bring solutions to your community.

Practical ways to encourage mentors

Hold meetings for mutual encouragement.

I recommend periodic meetings of all the mentors and the coordinator. At these meetings, mentors can trade stories and encourage each other. The coordinator may wish to arrange for motivational speakers to make presentations. All mentors should share victory reports with their fellows.

Mentors need mentors too!

Mentors need to be encouraged by regular conversations with people more spiritually mature than they are. This will help them put problems into perspective and see the big picture. When mentors encounter problems with their protégés, encourage them to seek wise counsel from pastors, child specialists, or wise older men.

Remind mentors that seeds take time to grow.

It's part of the nature of mentoring that you can't immediately detect progress. Often young people don't realize until later how they've benefited from the experience. Don't let mentors get discouraged because of a lack of immediate response from the boys.

A couple of years ago, I mentored a sixteen-year-old boy who dropped out of my group after only four weeks. He had met an older woman, and his attention was diverted from the mentoring effort. I saw this boy later in the mall. He gave me a hug in public, a sure sign that I had made some impact on him. But until I saw him in the mall that day, I had no idea!

Get the support of the mentor's wife.

The mentoring effort may be misunderstood by the mentor's wife. A man may not be doing all he could be at home, and the wife may view that hour or ninety minutes as time stolen from her and the family. I often tell wives that if they allow their husbands time to mentor children in need, a blessing will come to their homes. As a man sows good seed into the life of a child, that same seed will multiply and come back to his house.

As a man sows good seed into the life of a child, that same seed will multiply and come back to his house.

Giving spiritual encouragement

It has been my experience that mentoring is just as spiritually challenging as going door-to-door to tell others about Jesus. Most men who mentor will be thrust into a new level of spiritual warfare and will need additional support.

Journaling

I have seen men who seemed spiritually mature crumble two weeks into the mentoring effort. I encourage all men to keep journals of their struggles while mentoring. These journals will become records of the enemy's attempts to hinder them and of God's strong hand of deliverance in their lives.

Growing

Positive, productive ministry comes at a price. Problems are part of the mentoring effort, and they can't be avoided! I encourage men to see problems as opportunities for growth. The men who have consistently mentored are spiritual giants compared to who they were before they began. Their consistency has benefited the kingdom of God and their local churches.

Praying

Before implementing a church-based mentoring program, the church should seek to engage a large segment of the congregation in the ministry through prayer. Prayer partners can pray specifically for each mentor and his boys. The mentor should communicate weekly or monthly with his prayer partners to update them on progress and to make specific prayer requests.

Reading Scripture

Encourage the mentors to read these Scriptures when they need encouragement: Psalm 68:5; Proverbs 11:30; Isaiah 1:17; Matthew 25:34-40; 28:19-20; Luke 1:37; 11:9; Romans 1:16; 5:8; 2 Corinthians 10:4; 2 Timothy 1:7; Hebrews 6:10; and Revelation 20:11-15.

The role of the Holy Spirit

Not too long ago, a fifty-five-year-old man joined our church. Later as we talked, he made an interesting statement. He said he had decided to come home. He became aware that God was calling him back to the truth he had learned as a child in Sunday school.

As I reflected on the large number of young people who are unchurched, I realized that when they reach fifty-five years of age, there will be no spiritual home for them to go back to because they never were in Sunday school. They won't have any early childhood memories of singing in the children's choir and hearing about David and Goliath.

> *There will be no spiritual home for them to go back to because they never were in Sunday school.*

The Talks curriculum is built on the promise in Isaiah 55:11: "So is my word that goes out from my mouth: It will not return to me empty, but will accomplish what I desire and achieve the purpose for which I sent it." I sincerely believe that if we can share Scripture with young people and show how it relates to daily life, God will get involved in their lives. At the appropriate time, God will use the same Word that was shared with a young boy to draw a man to himself.

With the role of the Holy Spirit and God's Word in mind, a mentor should never feel discouraged. Remind the mentor that it isn't for him to determine the outcome based on what he can see. He can only stand firm on the fact that he shared God's Word and then trust God to do the work.

Some Important Issues

The ages of protégés

I recommend approaching boys in elementary or middle school for this ministry—while they're still easily impressed with adult men. I currently am mentoring third-graders, and they're much more open than boys in high school.

I'm discouraged that many single mothers don't bring their boys to church while they're still young instead of waiting until they're teenagers and in trouble and then seeking a miracle from the church. We're watching young men pass from youth to adulthood without ever being challenged by the wisdom of an older man. My favorite thesis statement is this: Every boy needs a man in his face, challenging him with wisdom regarding critical issues and decisions in his life.

Cross-cultural mentoring

Mentoring has many benefits that can impact society as a whole. One is cross-cultural communication. I assigned several white men to mentor black boys. This was a great experience for the boys and the men. One man told me he had been impacted by the boys and had gained an understanding of them. In every case, the men who hung in there had positive reports after it was over.

> *Every boy needs a man in his face, challenging him with wisdom regarding critical issues and decisions in his life.*

I can't deny that cross-cultural mentoring is difficult. Some men couldn't handle the challenge and dropped out. Each time this happened, I spoke with the man to find out why he stopped. In some cases the reason was legitimate, but in other cases I believe the cross-cultural effort was simply too much.

Of all the boys who were mentored cross-culturally, only one has rejected the idea. We make cross-cultural mentoring more palatable by approaching mentoring efforts as business agreements. We tell the boys that they aren't required to love their mentors. All we ask them to do is conduct business with their mentors: Read the chapters, answer the questions, and discuss the quotations. I often tell young men that if they're strong, they should be able to conduct business with mentors. This has been successful.

Mentoring in public schools

As I was speaking to a white middle school principal one day, she stated that she had heard the African proverb, "It takes a whole village to raise a child." She looked at me and said, "I have the children; where is the village?" I was stunned and ashamed. As I walked the halls of the school, I could only agree with her. Her cutting statement has been part of my motivation to get men and boys together in mentoring relationships. I charge local churches to lead the effort because of the strength we have through our relationship with Jesus.

I was a school teacher during the eighties, and I remember how difficult it was at that time for Christian men to interact with their local public schools. Now after years of deteriorating morals, uncontrollable students, student flight to Christian schools, and studies showing the value of religion in successful child-raising, public schools are once again talking to churches.

The door of opportunity is open for churches to be salt and light in the public school system. Every time I think of the opportunities to impact young people in a positive way, I get excited. The success of any endeavor of this kind depends on a person who will sacrifice personal time to make it happen.

> *We tell the boys that they aren't required to love their mentors. All we ask them to do is conduct business with their mentors.*

Networking

My church is a two-hour drive from three major cities. I've contacted churches in those areas who have a passion to impact the lives of young men, and together we've developed a network of churches with mentoring ministries. From time to time, two churches will meet for a Saturday fellowship. This encourages the mentors and also serves as an incentive to the boys.

The boys are driven to another city to spend time with boys from another church. Once we arrive at the host church, the boys take part in a Bible-based lesson that relates to them. We then involve the boys in an activity (usually basketball). My city is the site of a major university, so we always include a tour of the university.

These visits accomplish several things:

The boys are in a church environment all day.

While we're in the van, we seek to create a church environment, playing contemporary gospel music in the tape player. Many of these boys aren't familiar with church or with the peace that comes from the presence of God.

Adults learn more about the boys.

When young people ride in a bus or van, the driver becomes a "nonperson." In other words, young people act as if the driver isn't there. They speak freely, and this is an opportunity for adults to understand more about what's going on in the lives of young people.

The boys are exposed to positive peer pressure.

I see future deacons, ministers, and evangelists in each group of boys. I encourage them to act out their calling and be positive examples for others. Positive peer pressure is a wonderful tool in the hands of a mentor.

The boys see that God is a global God.

Too often, boys think of God as a local deity. They aren't aware that he has people everywhere. By visiting other churches, they learn that God is everywhere.

The boys become more acclimated to your church as their church home.

The boys begin to feel that your church is their church because of the time and money you invest in them. Actually the investment isn't that burdensome. It takes only two men from the visiting church to take the boys to another city, and the host church can entertain them with a minimum of two men.

Parting Thoughts

All my life I have heard the song "We Shall Overcome" as I grew up during the civil rights struggle. It was the battle cry of the black community. I was impressed with the unity of people struggling to overcome wickedness in our society. Today our entire society needs that same unity as we face the destruction of a whole generation of young men. The old battle cry can be modified for our contemporary crisis: "We Shall Save Our Youth." The challenge is to help society see the need and decide to get involved in the struggle.

My dad was a coal miner for many years. One day as he and the other men came up out of the hole, the foreman called them and said, "Come on, boys, we need to push this train."

My dad looked in front of him and saw a full-size coal car that needed to be moved. The men knew that this train weighed tons, but they knew they had to push the coal car. They surrounded the car until there wasn't a vacant spot around the perimeter. When the foreman gave the word, every man began to push on his spot, and a phenomenal thing happened. The coal car moved!

The coal miners were impressed. Before that day, none of them would have believed that men could push a coal car. Today we have a coal car in our neighborhoods that needs to be pushed. It won't move with a few professionals (school teachers, coaches, police) pushing the car. Men of the community must join together, completely surround the car, and push! When we do, we'll turn our young people, our communities, and our nation around.

Endnotes

[1] Richard John Neuhaus, "The Public Square," First Things, 65.

By Mark A. Holmen

Associate in Ministry at Trinity Lutheran Church in Stillwater, Minnesota, and Associate at The Youth and Family Institute of Augsburg College in Minneapolis, Minnesota

Lenten Faith Mentoring
Using Mentoring in Confirmation

Background for Lenten Faith Mentoring

While the concept of mentoring is not new, effective models or approaches for congregational mentoring are sometimes hard to come by. While at Gethsemane Lutheran Church in Hopkins, Minnesota, Pastor Steve Gartland developed a Faith Mentoring program to link teens in confirmation with adults they could engage in a series of guided, meaningful discussions around issues of faith. This mentoring program grew out of the desire to address two of the issues raised in the 1990 Search Institute report "Effective Christian Education: A National Study of Protestant Congregations."

Using the responses of more than eleven thousand participants of six denominations in 561 congregations throughout the United States, the report found a direct relationship between the maturity level of faith in teenagers and children and their opportunities to discuss faith issues with their parents and other adults. The more mature the level of faith in the children or teenagers, the more likely they were able to engage in meaningful conversations with adults about their faith.[1]

In another study, Search Institute surveyed more than 270,000 young people in six hundred communities and identified thirty assets necessary for success—good things that all young people need in their lives. These good things are crucial to the development of healthy, successful young people.[2] Two of the assets recognize the need for adult mentors in the lives of youth:

Asset four: other adult resources

"Kids have other adults besides their parents they can turn to for advice and support. Ideally, three or more adults play this role in their lives." Forty-nine percent of the young people surveyed reported having this asset in their lives.[3]

> *Effective models...for congregational mentoring are sometimes hard to come by.*

Asset five: other adult communication

"Kids have frequent, in-depth conversations with adults who are not their parents." Forty-one percent of the young people reported having this asset in their lives.[4]

In both cases, fewer than half the young people surveyed had meaningful relationships with adults besides their parents. Pastor Gartland and I set out to change this through mentoring.

Putting the Program in Place (and Seeing the Results!)

Fewer than half the young people surveyed had meaningful relationships with adults besides their parents.

It's not uncommon for the relationships that develop between adult mentors and teenagers to continue on their own well after the official end of the mentoring program.

The results of the Lenten Faith Mentoring program were overwhelming.

After considering several models of mentoring, Pastor Gartland added a Faith Mentoring segment to each year of the basic three-year confirmation program at his church. The mentoring program was added during the season of Lent while regular confirmation classes were suspended. This welcome addition to the confirmation class cycle not only provided a fresh change of pace in curriculum, but also helped keep confirmation students closely connected to the church through the season of Lent. The Faith Mentoring program proved to be very successful by many standards, not the least of which was the enthusiasm of confirmation teens and their adult mentors!

It's not uncommon for the relationships that develop between adult mentors and teenagers to continue on their own well after the official end of the mentoring program.

When Pastor Gartland moved to a new church, the mentoring program made the move as well. As the director of confirmation, I continued to develop the program by writing guided discussions between teenagers and mentors and integrating them with the Lenten worship service themes. I also added portrayals of biblical characters as the "sermons" for the midweek Lenten worship services. The program encourages the mentors and confirmands to worship together and then to go through thirty- to forty-minute guided discussions on faith and life issues using the discussion guides provided.

The results of the Lenten Faith Mentoring program were overwhelming. One result was a dramatic increase in the midweek Lenten worship attendance. Although we didn't anticipate these dramatic increases in attendance, they're now easy to understand. Besides the normal Lenten worship participants, we were adding confirmands, mentors, and parents of confirmands (junior highers can't drive themselves to church!).

Don't be mistaken—Lenten Faith Mentoring is first and foremost about building significant faith-sharing relationships between adults and young people. In those relationships, teenagers and adults have the opportunity to share with and learn from each other as fellow members of the Body of Christ.

A program like Lenten Faith Mentoring can breathe new life into your confirmation and Lenten ministries. Be prepared for more people to participate, and be creative with your worship planning because for many, this will be their first Lenten experience.

The Lenten Faith Mentoring plan is available from the Youth and Family Institute of Augsburg College. The resource includes discussion guides, bulletin announcements, time lines, and everything else you need to get this program going. It comes in manual form and also includes a computer disk so you easily can add information specific to your congregation. In fact, this program can be adapted to specific youth ministry programs and used apart from the Lenten season or even confirmation. Some churches use the model for a six-week period on Sunday mornings.

Be prepared for more people to participate.

Why Lent?

Lent is a great season that sets up Holy Week and the Easter celebration. Lent is also a great time for mentoring as it offers a short, six-week commitment opportunity for adults to try mentoring. And the mentoring program can be built into a midweek confirmation or other junior high ministry program. The season of Lent is a time of repentance, and midweek Lenten services usually offer a quiet, reflective style of worship. This style of worship establishes a good atmosphere for mentoring.

Lent offers a short, six-week commitment opportunity for adults to try mentoring.

Although the program is designed to be used during Lent, the discussion questions and basic model could be used at any time of year. The model is an "excelLent" short-term mentoring program with long-term results.

Character Portrayals

An optional segment of the Lenten Faith Mentoring program is a collection of character portrayals to be used in place of sermons for the Lenten worship services. These twenty- to thirty-minute character portrayals are dramatic presentations of biblical characters such as Pontius Pilate, Barabbas, Mary, Martha, and Judas.

These character portrayals breathe life into characters many people have read about for years.

These character portrayals breathe life into characters many people have read about for years. Replacing a sermon with these character portrayals is a great way to provide discussion material for mentors and youth and to engage the whole congregation—which will include junior high young people, mentors, parents, and the faithful Lent worshippers—in meaningful worship experiences.

Character Portrayals for Lent includes portrayals of Old Testament characters as well as New Testament characters and is available through the Youth and Family Institute of Augsburg College.

Getting Started

One of the keys to an effective mentoring program is preparation. The more time we spend in the planning stages, the better prepared we will be during the implementation stages. To help your congregation prepare for a confirmation-based mentoring program, take the following steps:

Step one: Educate and get the support of your church leadership.

It's important that your church leaders understand the need for mentoring and support the program you'll be initiating. In many cases, these will be your first volunteers for mentors!

Step two: Secure a mentor coordinator.

> *It's important to identify a key leader for this mentoring ministry.*

It's important to identify a key leader for this mentoring ministry. The mentor coordinator serves as the "point person," coordinating many of the important behind-the-scenes details. A mentor coordinator should be a task- and detail-oriented person who will commit to working with the program from October through April, if your program will take place during Lent. The heaviest time commitment will be in the month prior to Ash Wednesday.

Step three: Follow the time line.

A time line helps guide the coordinator through the program. Following the time line will keep anyone on task and on top of the details that need to be covered.

Some of the details in the Lenten Faith Mentoring time line include these:

- Use the mentor recruitment bulletin announcements (see the sample on page 65).
- Put together and distribute consideration packets.
- Track mentor pairings.
- Make copies of the discussion guides.
- Mail the mentor orientation letters.
- Mail the mentor wrap letters.
- Collect and process evaluations.

BULLETIN ANNOUNCEMENT

KIDS NEED TRUSTED ADULTS!

We need mentors to take part in the youth ministry program at our church. The mentoring program pairs individual young people with individual adults in our congregation in order to give them a forum to discuss faith and life issues.

A mentor plays an important role in the "gelling" process of a young person's growth in faith. No special training or background is required of a faith mentor other than a life of integrity and attendance at the mentor orientation. During the mentoring program, each faith mentor will meet with his or her student after services to discuss specific ways to relate the Christian faith to everyday life.

Young people need adults in addition to their parents with whom they can talk about faith and life issues. They need people like you—adults they can trust; adults with whom they can talk; adults who will listen; adults who are not afraid of sharing their own experiences, struggles, and dreams in putting Christianity into practice in the real world.

If you would like to be a mentor, please call the church office or the mentor coordinator. For more information about the mentor program, pick up a consideration packet in the church office.

Recruiting Mentors

I like to give junior high young people the opportunity to select their own mentors.

The sample bulletin announcement on page 65 is designed to solicit adults who would like to participate in the mentor program. While young people in the confirmation program are asked to find their own mentors, some young people will need help finding mentors. I like to give junior high young people the opportunity to select their own mentors. We do require them to find mentors who are at least twenty-one years old, members of the congregation, and not related to them. The adults who express interest as a result of these bulletin announcements are willing mentors your mentor coordinator can pair with the young people who are struggling to find mentors. The bulletin announcements also build awareness for the mentoring program among the members of your congregation.

Mentor Consideration Packets

The question adults ask most often regarding the mentor program is, "What do I have to do as a mentor?"

Realizing that time is the most precious commodity in today's world, it's important that we make clear what we're asking people to do in the mentoring program. People need to know what they're "getting themselves into" and how much time it will require of them. The question adults ask most often regarding the mentor program is, "What do I have to do as a mentor?"

To help people understand the requirements and responsibilities of the mentoring program, congregations can put together consideration packets.

A recommended consideration packet would include
- a cover letter to students, explaining their responsibilities;
- a cover letter to mentors, encouraging them to participate;
- a brief explanation of the program and how it will work;
- an outline of the mentor selection process;
- characteristics a mentor should have;
- training and screening requirements for mentors;
- the purpose of the mentoring program;
- the responsibilities and role of faith mentors; and
- a schedule of Lenten service dates, times, and other details.

In my experience, I've found that the more thorough the consideration packet, the more willing and confident adults are to volunteer.

The consideration packet thoroughly outlines the vision and need for mentoring as well as provides the critical details such as dates, times, and the location of the program. In my experience, I've found that the more thorough the consideration packet, the more willing and confident adults are to volunteer.

The consideration packets may be distributed in the following ways:
- Each participating young person receives a packet to give to the person he or she wants as a mentor.
- Consideration packets are given to any adults who respond to the bulletin

announcements or temple talks (see below).

● Extra consideration packets are available in the church office or hospitality center for anyone who is interested in the program.

Consideration packets, bulletin announcements, and temple talks will make your recruitment process for mentors much easier. What's a temple talk? Temple talks are the most powerful recruitment tool I've found. During these talks, young people and adults share personal feelings about mentoring. When a young person says, "I would like to have an adult besides my parents that I can talk to," you'll have adults standing in line to be mentors. These three recruitment tools will enable your young people to be successful in their search for mentors, and they'll help your adults understand what's being asked of them as mentors.

Don't Forget the Parents

Before I outline the mentor orientation program, I want to emphasize the importance of the parents' participation in the mentoring program. Parenting young people has never been easy; in today's increasingly fast-changing world, parenting has become even more difficult. Developmentally, teenagers are searching for their own identity, and part of this search drives them to explore life for themselves, away from their parents. In my conversations with parents, I have referred to this as a need for "healthy distancing."

Parenting young people has never been easy; in today's increasingly fast-changing world, parenting has become even more difficult.

Unfortunately what we see in many cases is *unhealthy* distancing between teenagers and their parents. For example, a recent episode of a daytime TV talk show was titled "I Want to Divorce My Eleven-Year-Old" and showcased an extreme example of how strained a relationship can become between parents and their children.

It's important for parents to understand that your mentoring program is not designed to be a "parent bashing" program. Parents are expected to participate in the mentor orientation, where they'll learn what the young people and mentors will be talking about. Parents are also expected to participate in a "mentor wrap" following the six weeks of mentoring to "reconnect" and hear about some of the experiences that were shared. It's critically important for the parents to understand what will be happening (mentor orientation), as well as what did happen (mentor wrap). While the Lenten Faith Mentoring program seeks to provide Christian adult role models for young people, in many cases the adult mentors become new resources for families.

In many cases the adult mentors become new resources for families.

Mentor Orientation

At this point all your young people have found mentors, and the program is ready to begin! The Lenten Faith Mentoring manual outlines a mentor orientation session designed for the young people, their parents, and mentors to attend so everyone can have a clear understanding of what will happen over the next six weeks.

The mentor orientation section of the Lenten Faith Mentoring manual provides

- a mentor orientation self-mailer letter,
- the purposes and goals of Lenten Faith Mentoring (can be used as an overhead),
- the responsibilities and role of faith mentors,
- meeting guidelines for mentors,
- "test run" discussion questions (can be used as an overhead), and
- a plan for a mentor commissioning service.

To get the program off to a good start, the mentor orientation covers the following areas:

Purpose

It's important that everyone involved—parents, young people, and mentors—understands the purposes for the mentoring program. These goals are

- to expand the circle of adults young people trust,
- to give every young person the opportunity to learn from an adult,
- to provide personalized learning so young people may verbalize their own faith, and
- to broaden adult participation in confirmation.

Plan

During this portion of the mentor orientation, you'll spend time discussing when mentors and young people will meet, where they'll meet, how long the meetings will last, and what happens if someone can't make one of the meetings. This is what I call the "details" portion of the orientation. It's important that the parents know and agree on the times for these meetings. The preferred plan is that the young people and the mentors attend the Lenten worship services together (sit together) and then follow their discussion guides immediately following the service. Some churches offer a Lenten supper before the service, which can also provide a good time for mentors to meet with young people.

Precautions

This portion of the orientation includes a list of meeting guidelines which are intended to help both mentors and young people establish and enjoy meetings in a safe environment of openness, trust, and honesty.

The church is becoming known as the only institution without screening procedures in place.

Preparation

At this time the discussion guides are handed out and you're ready to begin.

Practice

Mentors and young people participate in a short "test run" discussion to get to know each other. This first discussion time includes the parents.

Prayer

A final component of the mentor orientation is a commissioning service, which can be held at the end of the orientation program but is best suited for a worship service. It's important for the congregation to recognize and pray for those who are participating in the mentor program.

What About Screening Mentors?

It's important that we cover one more area before moving on. Unfortunately, in today's world we're faced with an increasing number of incidents of child molestation and sexual abuse. The church must face this reality and the danger that exists in any program that places young people in the care of adults. The church as an institution normally trusts the adults who come to us as volunteers, hesitating to ask questions.

This must change. The church is becoming known as the only institution without screening procedures in place. Those looking to molest children have a predator mentality, and they're seeking places where they can have one-to-one relationships with children. This is a compelling reason for screening adults who are interested in being mentors.

What will people think if we require screening procedures? Won't such procedures prevent some people from volunteering? Several years ago, there was some hesitancy from volunteers regarding the need for screening, but now this attitude has changed. Parents and adult volunteers are wondering why the church isn't screening adults. I have asked more than one thousand volunteers, "Would you be angry or would you not volunteer for a church program if you had to go through a screening process first?" The answer has been unanimous: "No."

I wish I could include a screening procedure in the Lenten Faith Mentoring manual, but screening must be handled by each congregation individually. Churches need to develop screening procedures that they're comfortable with and that encompass all their ministries to children and teenagers. One of the sources I recommend to congregations is *Reducing the Risk of Child Sexual Abuse in Your Church,* published by Church Law and Tax Report. Another is *The Good Shepherd Program: Tools to Protect Your Church by Preventing Child Abuse.* This is published by NEXUS Solutions in Fort Collins, Colorado.

Let the Mentoring Begin!

The Lenten Faith Mentoring manual includes three sets of six-session discussion guides. These were included to accommodate congregations using the mentoring program as a part of their three-year confirmation ministry. In most cases, the teenagers

> *It's important for the congregation to recognize and pray for those who are participating in the mentor program.*

> *Churches need to develop screening procedures that they're comfortable with and that encompass all their ministries to children and teenagers.*

and mentors will stay together for all three years. That's why three sets of discussion guides are necessary.

Each discussion guide begins with three questions focusing on the character portrayal from the Lenten service; if a congregation chooses not to do character portrayals, these questions can be eliminated.

● What was something I learned about tonight's character?
● Something I would like to ask this character is?
● How am I similar/different from the character?

From that point, the discussion guides focus on three well-known Scripture passages.

Set one—Matthew 28:19-20

"Therefore go and make disciples of all nations, baptizing them in the name of the Father and of the Son and of the Holy Spirit, and teaching them to obey everything I have commanded you. And surely I am with you always, to the very end of the age."

The six discussion themes for this set are "Go," "Disciples," "Baptism," "Trinity," "Teaching," and "I Will Be With Youth Always."

Set two—John 3:16

"For God so loved the world that he gave his one and only Son, that whoever believes in him shall not perish but have eternal life."

The six discussion themes for this set are "God," "World," "Jesus and Children," "Belief," "Perish," and "Eternal Life."

Set three—Romans 3:22-24

"This righteousness from God comes through faith in Jesus Christ to all who believe. There is no difference, for all have sinned and fall short of the glory of God, and are justified freely by his grace through the redemption that came by Christ Jesus."

The six discussion themes for this set are "Righteousness," "Faith," "Sin," "Justification," "Grace," and "Redemption."

As I was determining how to format the discussion guides so they would help stimulate meaningful discussion, a Star Trek theme came into my mind: "to boldly go where no one has gone before." That's it! That's what I have in mind with these mentoring discussions. In their conversations with one another, I would like young people and adults to spend time going where they've never gone before. So being a Star Trek fan, I used Star Trek terms to format and categorize the discussion guides. Let me explain.

Impulse power

This is the safe and easy speed for the Starship Enterprise. The first few questions are basic starter questions that are easy to answer and that will get the discussion moving at a safe speed.

Warp speed

When the Enterprise kicks into warp speed, the crew has decided where it's going, and it's time to *get going*. The warp speed questions will get the discussion turned toward the theme and in the direction of spiritual life and faith.

Maximum warp

The Enterprise is going all out. The maximum warp questions require sharing on a deeper level with no holding back.

After these theme-oriented questions, each discussion guide has a closing prayer that can be used to conclude each session. The prayers were intentionally formatted to be open-ended, allowing for individual intercessions. Be sure to cover this in your training, with an example of how mentors and young people are to pray together.

The discussion guides are reproducible, so you can make as many copies as you need. On the following page is a sample discussion guide.

Sample Discussion Guide

"Make Disciples"

"Therefore go and *make disciples* of all nations, baptizing them in the name of the Father and of the Son and of the Holy Spirit, and teaching them to obey everything I have commanded you. And surely I am with you always, to the very end of the age"

(Matthew 28:19-20).

Character Portrayal Discussion

What was something I learned about tonight's character?
Something I would like to ask this character is?
How am I similar/different from the character?

Impulse Power

1. Who is/was your favorite cartoon character and why?
2. Who is someone you respect/look up to/want to be like? Why?

Warp Speed

3. What are some qualities a role model should have?
4. Are you or have you ever been a role model for someone? Who? Would you like or did you like being a role model? Why or why not?
5. What are some of the qualities/characteristics of a disciple? How would they act, what would they do?

Maximum Warp

6. Who are some Christian disciples living today? Name some disciples who are known throughout the world. Name some disciples who are known in your church or community.
7. What are some ways that I act like a disciple of Christ?
8. What are some ways that I don't act like a disciple of Christ?
9. What are some things I could do to be a better disciple?

Closing Prayer

Dear Lord, we thank you for the disciples from our past and for the disciples that surround us today. Please help us to be better disciples by…Amen.

Mentor Wrap

The mentor wrap is the concluding event of the mentoring program. Young people, parents, and mentors are asked to attend this event which provides an opportunity for sharing, evaluation, presenting ongoing opportunities, and closure.

The *sharing* portion of the mentor wrap provides an opportunity for parents to connect with some of the experiences that were shared through the mentoring program. Participants generally share thoughts such as "When we first got together, I remember thinking..." "One of the most interesting things I learned about you is..." and "A way that you have helped me is..."

The *evaluation* is important so the leaders can continue to strengthen the program for the future. It also provides great feedback and "word bytes" for newsletters and other publicity. An evaluation form is provided in the manual.

Presenting ongoing opportunities is important for those who want to keep meeting. I'll never forget hearing this question at my first mentor wrap: "What if we don't want to quit meeting together? Do you have any resources for us to keep going?" The manual includes a list of suggested resources for ongoing mentoring.

The *closure* is probably the most powerful part of the program, as it's a time of celebration and thanksgiving for the relationships that were built. The rite-of-closure worship service provides a meaningful offering activity that has many times brought young people and adults to tears as they shared their feelings for each other. A complete outline for the closure service is included in the manual.

The mentor wrap portion of the Lenten Faith Mentoring manual includes
- a mentor wrap memo letter to parents, young people, and mentors;
- a mentor wrap welcome sheet (can be used as an overhead);
- a mentor wrap agenda;
- a rite-of-closure service outline;
- a sharing-activity plan (can be used as an overhead);
- a thanksgiving-activity plan (can be used as an overhead);
- a mentor program evaluation; and
- a list of resources for ongoing mentoring.

The Lenten Faith Mentoring program is an integral part of our confirmation program. For many of the young people, the mentoring is their favorite part of confirmation. Junior highers desperately need adults with whom they can talk and feel comfortable. Lenten Faith Mentoring has engaged our whole congregation in confirmation, and better yet, in the lives of junior high young people.

> *The evaluation is important so the leaders can continue to strengthen the program for the future.*

> *For many of the young people, the mentoring is their favorite part of confirmation.*

Endnotes

[1] *Effective Christian Education: A National Study of Protestant Congregations* (Minneapolis, MN: Search Institute, 1990), 4, 41.

[2] Peter L. Benson, Ph.D., Judy Galbraith, M.A., and Pamela Espeland, *What Kids Need to Succeed* (Minneapolis, MN: Search Institute and Free Spirit Publishing Inc., 1995), 2-3.

[3] Benson, et al., *What Kids Need to Succeed,* 32.

[4] Benson, et al., *What Kids Need to Succeed,* 35.

By Mary Somerville

National Coordinator for Mentor Moms with Young Life, and Local Director of Mentor Moms in Visalia, California

Women Supporting Young Women

Mentoring as Ministry to Teenage Mothers

"I wanted to get pregnant!" recalls high school senior Marcella. "All my friends were having babies. I thought it was cool and would get me out of the house. My friends were getting welfare and getting on their own, but I didn't have a clue what I was getting into! I thought it would be easier, like baby-sitting."

"I was definitely hysterical when I found out that I was pregnant!" recalls Cindy. "No one would understand. My boyfriend was long gone. My parents were sure to kick me out, if not kill me. My friends would go on with their lives. I knew I'd be alone—alone with a baby to care for. I was right."

> "*I knew I'd be alone—alone with a baby to care for. I was right.*"
>
> **—Cindy**

"What hit me was that I'd let everyone down, including my parents and my friends at youth group and at church, and I wanted to kill myself!" recalls Christy. "What really surprised me was that my youth group and church have helped me beyond what I ever could have hoped for, and my parents too!"

Every year, about a million teenagers in the United States like Marcella, Cindy, and Christy, from various backgrounds and situations, become pregnant. What youth worker is not aware that teenage pregnancy is a national problem?

● "The United States continues to have the highest adolescent pregnancy, abortion, and birth rates in the industrialized world."[1]

● "Of all adolescent pregnancies occurring each year, it is estimated that approximately 50 percent end in birth, 35 percent end in abortion, and 14 percent end in miscarriage."[2]

● In 1996, there were 505,513 births to women under age twenty. In that same year, 76 percent of births to teenagers were to unmarried mothers.[3]

● More than 80 percent of pregnant teenagers report that their pregnancies are unintended.[4]

Most of them will struggle just to finish high school, struggle to hold down low-paying jobs, and struggle for the rest of their lives to create stable lives for themselves and their children.

What better opportunity could we have to point these young women to the cross of Christ?

It's crucial that anyone involved in the mentoring program sees this as more than just a social service; it's a ministry for God with eternal dividends.

Even without looking at the numbers, we know that teenage pregnancy affects our youth groups and churches. It's a problem the church must address.

These young mothers face enormous consequences. Most of them will struggle just to finish high school, struggle to hold down low-paying jobs, and struggle for the rest of their lives to create stable lives for themselves and their children.

The cycle of poverty and suffering is perpetuated from one generation to the next. But these consequences are our opportunities! What better opportunity could we have to point these young women to the cross of Christ? There they'll see Jesus bearing the penalty for their sins and the weight of their guilt. What better opportunity could we have to point them to the empty tomb? There they'll see the risen Savior who has conquered physical and spiritual death. These young women need to know that Jesus gives new, abundant life. He offers mercy and grace to help them, and he'll never leave them.

Laying the Groundwork

Before launching into a description of the mentoring program, I'd like to set forth the biblical principles that make the program necessary and keep it running. It's crucial that anyone involved in the mentoring program sees this as more than just a social service; it's a ministry for God with eternal dividends.

God's glory: our motive

Our highest calling is to display God's splendor. Paul set it before us: "So whether you eat or drink or whatever you do, do it all for the glory of God" (1 Corinthians 10:31). Jesus is worthy of universal praise and adoration. When we are consumed with his glory, no sacrifice is too great to make his glory known.

Jesus: our example

One of the best ways to display the glory of Christ is to imitate him. He reached out to the down-and-outs, the castoffs of his society, the downtrodden—the ones who saw themselves as sinners, not the self-righteous.

Teenage mothers fit this description. For the most part, they're down and out. If they're on their own, they live in poverty. They're looked down upon as a drain on our society. They're overburdened with raising their children, usually without the help of husbands. They're misfits in the teenage culture of a carefree lifestyle. Their sin is evident to everyone, and they can't deny it. There's no pretending to be righteous. That's why many continue in a promiscuous lifestyle.

Would Jesus have ministered to a teenage mother in his day? You bet! Look at Mary Magdalene, one of the recipients of his love and grace. Look at the woman caught in adultery. Look at the woman at the well. Jesus had the time to reach out to stigmatized women. His love changed them forever. We need his love flowing through us for the young woman who has "blown it." We need to be approachable. We need to be people exhibiting grace to the glory of God.

Some would say, "Shouldn't we let the teenage mom bear the consequences of her sin? Aren't we condoning her sin if we support and encourage her?" If we answer yes to these questions, we're refusing to offer the free grace that we have received from Jesus. When we give support and encouragement, we're mirroring the greater grace that has been given to us.

By getting involved with teenage mothers, we aren't condoning or minimizing their sin. Through our lifestyles of integrity, we can show them that righteousness is what truly satisfies. By our love and acceptance, we can show them that salvation comes through grace, not something we do. If they choose to respond to God's grace, they'll become new people in Christ.

The Great Commission: our orders

Jesus commissioned his followers to "go and make disciples of all nations" (Matthew 28:19). The meaning of the word "go" in the original text implies "as you go." As we go about our lives, we are sure to come into contact with teenage moms. If evangelism and discipleship are our priorities, we won't want to pass up this supreme opportunity to share the love of Christ. As we reach out to young mothers in their need, we'll win a hearing for the gospel.

Gratitude: our response

As Christians, we must never forget that we're recipients of God's grace. We can minister to others out of gratitude for the grace extended to us. But before we venture to help others, we need to examine our own hearts. Do we make light of our sins of pride, self-righteousness, favoritism, gossip, harsh words, selfishness, and lack of compassion?

When we realize that we're just beggars telling other beggars where to get bread, we're ready to minister the love and grace of Christ to teenage moms. The Apostle Paul spelled out our motivation: "For Christ's love compels us...he died for all, that those who live should no longer live for themselves but for him who died for them and was raised again" (2 Corinthians 5:14-15).

Would Jesus have ministered to a teenage mother in his day? You bet!

If evangelism and discipleship are our priorities, we won't want to pass up this supreme opportunity to share the love of Christ.

Believe that all things are possible through the power of the Holy Spirit.

When we get involved with teenage moms, we become more and more aware of the high price-tag sin carries.

> *God's Word provides the wisdom and confidence we need to speak loving truth to teenage mothers.*

> *"Mary, can you counsel with an unmarried friend of mine who had a baby and really needs help?"*

> *I've seen many lives changed over the past ten years as women like me have ministered one-to-one to hurting and needy teenage moms.*

The Holy Spirit: our power

We must trust God to work by the power of his Spirit. Then we must step out in faith and put our equipment to work. Sometimes we have to go beyond our comfort zones to minister the love of Christ when it seems pointless. Believe that all things are possible through the power of the Holy Spirit.

The Word of God: our wisdom

How do we deal with the ramifications of sin in the life of a teenage mother? When we get involved with teenage moms, we become more and more aware of the high price-tag sin carries. Many of these young women are dealing with emotional or physical abuse, in the past or the present. Some have had previous abortions or have had babies taken away from them. Some have been or still are addicted to drugs. Some have been in trouble with the law. Many are from broken homes. Many have been abandoned by their parents. They've been sinned against, and many are living lives of sin themselves. Others are rebels who have scorned all spiritual privileges. What good can we do?

These situations can be intimidating. We may feel helpless to relate or assist. Many of these girls need specialists with psychological training to understand and help troubled teenagers. There are times it's necessary to involve professionals, but only Jesus can give the real hope and help teenage mothers need to make necessary changes.

These girls need friends who can be strong examples for them, support them, and point them to Jesus. God's Word provides the wisdom and confidence we need to speak loving truth to teenage mothers.

Prayer: our key to victory

As described in Ephesians 6:10-18, we must be equipped with the spiritual tools we need. Prayer is key. Remember that God is working in the life of each teenage mom. At the same time, she is facing the consequences of her choices, and she may be struggling with the temptations of a sinful lifestyle.

Every step of faith she takes will be tested. Sometimes it seems that for every step forward, she takes two steps back. We must keep our faith strong and keep supporting the young woman in prayer.

Mentoring: a Strategy for Ministry

The author's background

"Mary, can you counsel with an unmarried friend of mine who had a baby and really needs help?" was the plea over the phone which started me on this ten-year adventure of ministering to teenage moms. My friend told me that this young woman was totally incapacitated, on about a dozen drugs and sitting around all day in despair. She hadn't seen her baby in two years.

I met with this young woman, pointing her back to her Good Shepherd and giving her hope and comfort. Many times my emotions told me to give it up; she was anything but lovable in her depression, her squalid house, and her dingy clothes. But the love paid off, and she made a commitment to Jesus. Her life began to change. We obtained a lawyer to plead her case, and she was granted visitation rights with her child as long as I was present.

For two years, I spent two hours a week with her and her child as they played together and established their relationship. Through the help of her doctor, she was able to get off drugs. She has lived out her faith ever since, establishing a good relationship with her child and the child's father. She still deals with the consequences of sin in her life, but she is able to glorify God.

That experience turned out to be a big investment of time for me.

Was it worth it? I believe it was!

Through that experience, I learned that those of us who know Jesus and trust him to change lives need to be involved in helping young women who need Christ. I've seen many lives changed over the past ten years as women like me have ministered one-to-one to hurting and needy teenage moms.

Six years ago I was approached by Young Life about setting up a program to reach teenage moms in our area, so I set up a one-to-one mentoring program. It has been my privilege to match 127 teenage moms to mentors in our program, which we call Mentor Moms. What a joy to see all those lives impacted for Jesus! There is no better way to minister to teenage moms than to provide the presence of caring women who can offer support, counsel, and friendship, and can be examples on a one-to-one basis. That's what mentoring is all about.

How does a caring woman come into the life of an unwed teenage mother? A woman with a burden for a teenage mother can do this on her own or can set up a mentoring program in a church, a youth group, or an organization.

Mentoring defined

A mentor is an experienced and trusted friend, a person who comes alongside as an adviser. In our context, a mentor is a nonparental adult woman who is concerned about a teenage mother and wants to serve Christ by reaching out to the teenager. It involves spending time with her to build the relationship. It involves talking to her as a friend, finding out her dreams and problems, and helping her find solutions. It involves encouraging her to set goals and believing that through Christ she can reach them. It involves opening one's life for her to observe and emulate. It may involve discipling her through a Bible study.

Mentoring is one-to-one

If teen pregnancy is such a huge problem—and it is—what good is it to touch such a small number of lives? Wouldn't it be better to get large numbers of these young women together and have a program for them?

This mentoring model is based on the belief that the world is changed one person at a time.

That may be effective in some cases, but the benefit of one-to-one mentoring over a group setting is that mentoring means spending more in-depth time with the teenager, yielding greater results. The needs of a teenage mom are so great that it's more beneficial to provide one-to-one attention.

This mentoring model is based on the belief that the world is changed one person at a time. As a mentor invests time and attention in a teenage mom's life and the child's life, she is affecting generations and making eternal investments in people's lives. It will be challenging and frustrating at times, but very rewarding. Jesus builds his church one person at a time. Individuals are important to him.

Steps to Setting up a Mentoring Program

1. Assess the need and the resources to meet the need.

Ask these questions: What is the need within your community, schools, and/or church? Will the project fit your church's or youth group's mission? What are your resources for meeting that need? Are there individuals with a burden for this ministry who would form an advisory committee? Do you want to go outside your church for the personnel to administer and staff the program? Do you need a full-time or part-time director? What qualifications do you want from a director? What experience? If the director is paid, how will that be funded? What are the costs of starting and maintaining the program? What do you want to call your program? How will you make it known? Who will promote it?

2. Set up an advisory committee.

A committee of interested individuals should meet together and discuss the preceding questions. It may take months for this committee to pray for God's wisdom and discuss everything involved. When they know God is leading them to begin, they should find a director to carry out the goals and objectives.

3. Secure a director.

The director should be a Christian woman with a burden to minister the love of Christ specifically to needy teenage mothers. She also should have good organizational skills, and Christian ministry experience would be helpful. Her job will be to recruit others to help her administrate and carry out the program. It's a good idea to ask for at least one or two years of commitment to this ministry.

4. Recruit mentors.

The director is responsible for recruiting mentors. A mentor must be a mature Christian woman with a burden for pouring her life into a single teenage mom. Mentors must also understand that mentoring is a big commitment.

The director and the advisory committee should decide where the mentors will be recruited from: within your own church or in the broader Christian community. The director will then talk to individuals

The background check is crucial to guarding against abuse.

or groups she thinks would be interested in this ministry—women's Bible study groups, Sunday school classes, and missions conferences, for example.

The director must decide what is required of mentors—training, time commitment, and length of ministry, for example. Interested women must be interviewed and screened. They should agree to a statement of faith your church is comfortable with. They should be fully supportive of the goals of the mentoring ministry and be willing to commit to the requirements, including attending training sessions and other activities. They should fill out applications and provide personal references.

It's also a good idea to require a prospective mentor to sign a sexual conduct statement, acknowledging that she is living a pure lifestyle—one free from sexual activity outside marriage. She should sign a statement agreeing that your church or organization may conduct a background check, which might include contacting previous employers, educational institutions, churches, and other organizations. You must also be able to check records of criminal arrests and convictions and civil judgments involving sexual assault, child abuse and molestation, sexual harassment, incidents of violence, and other unlawful conduct. The background check is crucial to guarding against abuse.

5. Recruit teenage moms.

The director is also responsible for interviewing teenage moms and explaining the program to them. If the teenage mom wants to be a part of the program, she should fill out an application, giving some information about herself.

The only criteria we've used for including young women in the program are that they must be single teenagers who are pregnant or are moms, and they must be open to having mentors. If a young woman gets married while she is in the program, we support it if we can, and we let her stay in the program. If a young woman turns twenty while she is in the program, we let her stay.

> *It's a good idea to start with the teenage mothers in your church.*

Recruiting from within the church

It's a good idea to start with the teenage mothers in your church. Hardly any church hasn't had to deal with teenage pregnancy. The program can begin with only one young woman. As this small program becomes successful, more will want to participate.

If the teenage mom already has a supportive family, a mentor is still of great benefit. Usually a family within the church that is supporting a daughter in her pregnancy welcomes another member of the church as help. The burden can be overwhelming; the more help and support, the better. However, at the outset of the relationship, the director or the mentor should talk to the mother of the teenage mom and explain the mentor's role. Usually the mother of the teenage mom welcomes another caring woman coming alongside her daughter.

Recruiting from outside the church

Some people in your church may say they don't want their children associating with sexually active young people from outside the church. While it's true that teenage moms have particular problems and needs that need to be addressed, they need to know that they're welcome in the church's youth program. What better way for them to see the love of Christ in action than to be welcome in the church? It's an opportunity for the youth group to display the love of Christ in tangible ways. The church should be a place for people to be forgiven and restored, not for self-righteous people to get together and thank God that they're not like the sinners. Jesus had a lot to say about that.

Recruiting teenage mothers from outside the church also provides an opportunity for the mentors to reach out to the young women's families.

High schools—You can recruit teenage moms from local high schools by presenting the program to a school administrator and asking for referrals. Administrators are looking to refer needy students to mentoring programs, and they'll usually welcome you even though your program is church-based. It's legal for schools to refer teenagers to your program since it's voluntary for the girls. Be sure you tell schools and young women up front that it's a Christian program.

Word of mouth—When the program becomes known, word gets around that your program offers help for pregnant teenagers and teenage moms. There are always more girls who want mentors than we have mentors for. We put young women on a waiting list as well as a prayer list until God supplies mentors.

As women reach across racial, generational, economic, cultural, and other differences in love, young women respond.

6. Match mentors and teenage moms.

When I match mentors and young women, I try to pair women of the same cultural or racial heritage if they're available. If not, I encourage the mentor to learn about the culture of her young woman by reading books written by authors who speak for that race or culture, listening to music from that culture, seeing people of that culture worship, and learning some of the language if applicable and possible. As women reach across racial, generational, economic, cultural, and other differences in love, young women respond.

When a match has been made, the director should meet with the mentor and the teenage mom together and present the expectations. She should encourage both to talk about their expectations for the relationship. She should remind both that friendships take time to grow and that they must be patient with each other. She should encourage the teenager to draw on the resources available through her mentor: asking questions, getting her mentor's input, and watching her mentor's life.

It's important at this point to set up a way for the two women to get in touch with each other. Then they should set up a time to get together again, and they embark on this wonderful mentoring adventure.

7. Train the mentors.

Women entering this program will want training and encouragement in this new role. They'll want to know how to reach out to their teenage moms and how to most effectively show them the love of Christ.

Preparatory training

The director must decide how much training the mentors need prior to matching. In our program, the initial interview with the director covers the orientation needed for beginning as a mentor. In that session, I define mentoring and outline the goals of the program. We talk about expectations. I emphasize commitment to the relationship on a regular basis, and I assure them of my ongoing support, counsel, and training.

If you want to offer more preparatory training, you must decide how often you will offer it and what topic areas you'll cover. You must also determine who will conduct the training. You may want to bring in experts such as youth workers, pastors, labor coaches, obstetricians, crisis pregnancy counselors, Christian counselors and social workers, and experienced mentors.

Mentor Training Goals

- To remind mentors of the biblical basis for what we're doing
- To stress positive character qualities in the mentors' lives
- To train mentors on how to share their faith
- To share wisdom in dealing with difficulties teenage mothers face
- To remind mentors that success is loving the girls by meeting consistently
- To help mentors deal with seeming failure when they get no response
- To provide helpful resources for mentors and their girls

In-service training

It has been my experience that the most beneficial training happens while the women are serving as mentors. For the most part, mentoring is unleashing the knowledge and experience the mentor already has. The program is effective only as the mentors share from their own life experiences and pass along the wisdom they have gained.

> *For the most part, mentoring is unleashing the knowledge and experience the mentor already has.*

Since the in-service training continues throughout the year, women can enter the program at any time. They plug right into the ongoing mentor meetings, where mentors study the Bible together, discuss mentoring issues and experiences, share wisdom, and pray. They also talk about ways to deepen their friendships with the young women, give them support, and challenge them.

In our program, we use a training manual I've compiled, which includes eighteen mentor training sessions. It's called *Mentor Moms: A Handbook for Mentoring Teenage Mothers*. (This book is available from the Young Life Service Center in Colorado Springs, Colorado.) Each training session lasts two hours.

8. Support the mentors.

Mentors need ongoing support and encouragement to prevent burnout and sustain their involvement. This support comes through in-service training meetings and phone calls from the director. I also send out monthly newsletters, letting mentors know how much they're appreciated and encouraging them with thoughts from God's Word. The

> *The teenage mom must see the love of Christ before she'll want to hear about it.*

newsletter also outlines the activities planned for the month and informs mentors of other related business.

9. Plan and coordinate activities for mentors and teenage moms.

The mentors and teenage moms participate in activities that are driven by the goals of the program: evangelism and discipleship.

Activities for evangelism

This program is set up for lifestyle evangelism. The teenage mom must see the love of Christ before she'll want to hear about it. The mentor builds the bridge of love and friendship to win a hearing for the gospel.

Friendship-building activities—Any activities that build friendship and show love are appropriate in this program. Mentors are creative, and I've seen them do all kinds of things with their girls, such as crafts, baking cookies, making picture albums, and making baby blankets. Other ideas include picnics in the park, trips to the zoo, evenings at home with the mentor's family, a wedding in the backyard, and a bridal shower or a baby shower.

Sharing the good news—The mentor's story of faith is the most effective means of reaching a young woman. The mentor should be able to share her faith, including Scriptures that show God's plan for bringing people to himself.

Other opportunities for evangelism—A mentor might want to take advantage of other opportunities such as Christian concerts, youth group activities, speakers, plays, church meetings, conferences, and women's retreats. Good books and articles are also helpful.

Activities for discipleship

Bible studies—One-to-one Bible study is an effective way to disciple a teenage mom. If the teenage mom is not open to a study with her mentor, encourage her to get involved in another study. Many church youth groups offer discipleship groups. Or if possible, get a group of Christian teenage moms together. Do a Bible study with them, and talk about issues they deal with.

Modeling and teaching—Apart from formal Bible studies, a mentor has continual opportunities to disciple her teenage mom. She can talk to her about—and perhaps model—child care. She can talk about the need to finish high school and work hard on her studies.

A club for teenage moms and mentors

> *Along with the one-to-one relationships, large groups are important.*

Along with one-to-one relationships, large groups are important. We set up a once-a-month club for all the teenage moms, babies, and their mentors. If the teenage moms are active in youth group, a club may not be necessary. The children are in the nursery during meetings. We always try to make the setting special for the girls, including table decorations, a theme, and a simple program.

Game or craft time—At the beginning of the meeting, we usually play a game. The game time breaks down barriers and shows the young women that the mentors are real people who like to have fun.

We sometimes replace the game with a craft such as baby hand prints in plaster of Paris, birthday banners, name signs, note cards, or Christmas ornaments.

Singing—If enough young women are present to sing comfortably, we sing a few praise choruses, accompanied by a guitar.

Message—The message should be relevant to the needs of the young women, giving biblical answers to problems they face. We often have women tell what Christ has done in their lives.

Recognitions—The teenage moms are recognized for accomplishments such as giving birth, graduating from school or training programs, and receiving awards. We always recognize the birthdays of young moms and their children.

Sharing and prayer—The young women share prayer requests, and the mentors pray. This is a great time of sharing and seeing God answer prayer.

Refreshments—We serve delicious refreshments and enjoy fellowship.

Share table—Sometimes we set up a table for baby clothes and other items the girls want to share with each other.

Showers

For young women outside the church—Mentors and other women within the church can and should host showers for teenage moms outside the church. They can invite women and teenagers from the church, making known that the goal for the showers is to show young women the love of Jesus.

For young women within the church—If young women ever need the support of their church families, they need it when they're about to become teenage mothers! One way the church can show her love and support is to give her a church shower. (For a thorough treatment of dealing with teenage pregnancy in the church, see my chapter, "Counseling Single Teenage Mothers" in *Women Helping Women,* Harvest House Publishers Inc., 1997, page 111.)

Other activities, outings, and camps

Another aspect of our outreach to teenage moms is taking the girls on trips as a group. We've provided everything from day trips to the beach to week-long or weekend camps. We've taken girls and their babies to the zoo, had picnics at the park, gone on a hayride followed by a bonfire, had swim parties, taken them to Christian concerts, put on plays for them, and baby-sat so the young women could go to a theme park for the day. These events all say, "We love you and want you to experience the joy we have in knowing Christ." At many of these events, we share what it means to have a relationship with Jesus.

10. Raise funds.

If this program is a ministry of the local church, it may be funded by the church. You may need to ask people in your congregation to sponsor your program in addition to their regular giving to the church.

If this ministry is sponsored by a parachurch organization or an individual, you'll need to raise funds. The director can coordinate this effort, working with others who want to help. You may want to ask churches to include this ministry in their missions giving. You also can ask companies to include this in their charitable giving. Sometimes grant money is available for this type of program.

The budget for this mentoring ministry will be different for each program, but you should consider these factors: the director's salary and expenses if applicable, office supplies, telephone expenses, printing, educational supplies for the mentors, club meetings, trips and outings, conferences for the director and the mentors, a rented meeting place if necessary, and camp scholarships.

11. Represent the ministry.

The sponsoring committee and director should represent the ministry to the church or any other supporting group. They should present an overview of the program in an effort to raise up mentors, financial support, and prayer support. The best way to present the ministry is to either relate what God has done in an individual's life or to have that woman share her story. I also like to make a video or slide presentation and to keep a scrapbook to show prospective mentors.

You may want to develop a brochure outlining the program. Distribute brochures during presentations, place them in churches, or leave them in other places to advertise the program. A brochure should include the name of the program, its purpose, what being a mentor involves, how teenagers are recruited, the benefits to young mothers, and a number to call for information.

12. Provide evaluation.

Ongoing evaluation is important for improving the program. The director should ask mentors what they think the ministry has done in the teenage mothers' lives. (See the sample evaluation on page 90.)

God will reward those who show the love of Christ to a needy teenage mom and her child, leaving the results in the hands of the one who loves them the most!

13. Reap eternal rewards.

God's Word tells us, "So neither he who plants nor he who waters is anything, but only God, who makes things grow. The man who plants and the man who waters have one purpose, and each will be rewarded according to his own labor" (1 Corinthians 3:7-8). It's unimportant which we do: plant or water or reap the crop. We're all workers for God's kingdom, and we'll share the rewards in eternity. If God rewards a person who gives a cup of cold water in Jesus' name, he'll reward those who show the love of Christ to a needy teenage mom and her child, leaving the results in the hands of the one who loves them the most!

Endnotes

[1] "Adolescent Pregnancy and Childbearing," Advocates for Youth (March 1996), taken from *The Best Intentions* (Washington, D.C.: National Academy Press, 1995).

[2] "Adolescent Pregnancy and Childbearing," Advocates for Youth (March 1996), taken from *Sex and America's Teenagers* (New York, NY: Alan Guttmacher Institute, 1994).

[3] "Facts at a Glance," Child Trends (October 1997).

[4] "Adolescent Pregnancy and Childbearing," Advocates for Youth (March 1996), taken from *The Best Intentions* (Washington, D.C.: National Academy Press, 1995).

Tips for Mentoring

SPIRITUAL AND EMOTIONAL ISSUES

- Be a good listener. Find out what's going on in your young woman's life and what her interests, desires, and problems are. If she's going through a trial, encourage her to talk about it and to see how God might be working in her life. Don't be afraid to talk about difficult issues such as sex.

- Don't hesitate to express your own personal values to your young woman. Let her know how important Christ is to you.

- Affirm her in all the things you can. Then reaffirm again. She needs someone to be positive about her. Praise her for the things she is doing right.

- Offer to take her to church with you. Help her if she struggles with leaving her child in the nursery.

- Let her help you in a service project. She'll learn the joy of serving.

- Help her deal with feelings of frustration and stress in mothering. If anger is a problem, help her deal with her anger appropriately.

- If she has trouble making decisions, talk about principles that will help her, using the Word of God as a guide, not the expectations of others.

SCHOOL ISSUES

- Help her learn how to do well in school. Teach her how to study for a test, take notes, use the library, use a computer, or understand a subject.

- Encourage her to do her homework, and help her if you can.

- Help her set goals for her grades, and encourage her in reaching them.

MOTHERING ISSUES

- Attend childbirth classes with her. If she wants you to, be there at the birth of her child or at least shortly afterward.

- Help her understand how to give loving, nurturing attention to her child. Give her tips on feeding and nutrition.

- Address child discipline as the child gets older.

- Help her with skills she'll need as a mother, such as cooking, menu planning, shopping, budgeting, hosting a birthday party, and making memories.

- Talk about the role of the father, and help her deal with issues that arise.

- Identify community resources for teenage moms, such as baby-sitting, so she can continue her education.

- Help her affirm her child by taking pictures of her child, making a picture album, praising her child, and talking to her child in a kind fashion.

CAREER ISSUES

- Give her a vision for what she can become. Talk about the lifestyle she wants, things she's good at, and what she dreams of. Help her construct some short- and long-range goals. Then talk about what she'll have to do to get there. Remind her that she may have to forestall immediate satisfaction.

- Present ideas to challenge and inspire her.

- If you're a working woman, take her to work and show her what you do.

- Find out her interests, and develop them through books and articles.

- Help her stay motivated to finish school in order to reach her goals.

- Encourage her to go to college or a trade school so she'll be equipped to support herself and her child.

Mentor Evaluation Form

Name of Mentor: _____

Name of Teenage Mom: _____

Dates of Mentoring Relationship: _____ to _____

If the mentoring relationship has been terminated, why?

What do you think has been accomplished through this ministry in the following areas of your

    teenage mom's life?

Spiritual life

Academics

Child

Career

Other

What was accomplished in your own life through this ministry?

What elements of the program would you like to keep as they are, and what would you change

    or delete?

How can we improve this ministry?

By Dr. Richard R. Wynn with Steve Gardner

President and Vice President of Emerging Young Leaders in Englewood, Colorado

A Modern Strategy Based on a First-Century Model

Mentoring as Leadership Training

Miss Thompson was an elementary school teacher. One year she had a student named Teddy Stallard. Teddy was troubled, often a source of frustration for Miss Thompson. He was a slow learner and showed little enthusiasm.

Miss Thompson had seen the records of Teddy's last four years in school. She remembered that during his first-grade year, Teddy had showed promise in terms of work and attitude, but his home life was poor. In the second grade, his mother had become seriously ill. During his third-grade year, she had died. During the last year, his home life had become increasingly unstable, his father showing no interest in Teddy's schoolwork. Life had become a mess for Teddy.

At Christmastime, Miss Thompson received gifts from the children in her class. Among the gifts, Miss Thompson was surprised to see a crudely wrapped gift from Teddy. She opened it and found a gaudy bracelet with some of the rhinestones missing and a half-empty bottle of cheap perfume. When the class began to laugh, Miss Thompson quickly put on the bracelet and some perfume, letting them know she really appreciated both gifts.

After class, Teddy lingered. "I'm glad you liked my gifts, Miss Thompson," he stammered. "And—you smell just like my mother did."

Miss Thompson immediately recognized that she was more than just a schoolteacher to Teddy. The gifts he had given her were the most prized treasures from his mother's belongings. The rest of the year she was amazed at how well he responded to her increased attention.

Teddy never forgot Miss Thompson. When he graduated from high school, he wrote to let her know that he was graduating second in his class. Four years later he wrote that he was graduating from the university, first in his class. The note that came in another four years said:

Dear Miss Thompson,

As of today I am Theodore Stallard, M.D. How about that? I wanted you to be the first to know. I am getting married next month, the 27th to be exact. I want you to come and sit where my mother would sit if she were alive. You are the only family I have now; Dad died last year.

Love,

Teddy Stallard

Miss Thompson wiped the tears from her eyes. She rightfully took the place of Teddy's mother at the wedding. She had been an invaluable mentor to him, believing in him when no one else did—changing his entire outlook on life.[1]

This is the kind of impact we all would like to have with young people, but we can't help asking ourselves whether we're moving in the right direction. We have to occasionally stand back and re-evaluate the big picture.

Is the status quo of youth ministry decaying under the weight of its own excesses? Do you ever feel the nagging suspicion that like TV, youth ministry has become entertainment-driven and content-light? Perhaps you've pioneered a major shift but struggle with the effectiveness of the delivery system. Do we need a new paradigm? Some say it's time for a revolution.

As you consider developing a mentoring program for your young people, you probably have at least three important questions at the very outset:

- Do I have to change ministry models again?
- Why mentoring?
- Is it worth the time and energy?

The answers, each in a word, are

- partly,
- results, and
- absolutely.

Do I Have to Change Ministry Models Again?

The operative word in this question is "change." The concept of change is emotionally charged. The following quote may even represent a soapbox on which you've stood.

> The world is too big for us. Too much going on, too many crimes, too much violence and excitement. Try as you will, you get behind in the race, in spite of yourself. It's an incessant strain, to keep pace...And still, you lose ground. Science empties its discoveries on you so fast that you stagger beneath them in hopeless bewilderment. The political world is news seen so rapidly you're out of breath trying to keep pace with who's in and who's out. Everything is high pressure. Human nature can't endure much more!"[2]

Although it sounds like a modern plea, the above paragraph is lifted from the June 16, 1833 edition of the Atlantic Journal. More than a century and a half later, we have become accustomed to more and even faster change. Some people relish it; others hate it; most resist it if it requires *them* to change.

Sydney Harris said, "Our dilemma is that we hate change and love it at the same time; what we want is for things to remain the same but get better."[3]

Even more to the point is this statement from a Harvard business school professor named Rosabeth Moss Kanter: "The individuals who will succeed and flourish will also be masters of change: adept at reorienting their own and others' activities in untried directions to bring about higher levels of achievement."[4]

Although the essence of our message (the gospel) is changeless and eternal, the methodology of youth ministry is constantly evolving. You can have one of three major responses to change:

You can fight it and be frustrated.

You can accept it and be adaptive.

You can lead it and be creative.

Like it or not, change is here to stay.

Emerging Young Leaders has devised a way to do mentoring that keeps the time and energy costs low and the benefits high—a way that doesn't require scrapping current youth programs in order to initiate the new. It requires some leadership on the part of the youth director at the outset, but the development of significant leadership in both students and adult volunteers during the process is a benefit that cannot be compared with the initial cost. And as most students of social trends will tell you, we are in the middle of a lack-of-leadership crisis.

> *"What we want is for things to remain the same but get better."*
>
> **—Sydney Harris**

Why Mentoring?

Bill LeTourneau, vice president of communications for Emerging Young Leaders (EYL), states it this way:

> "Faced with the prospect of having only three years to fulfill his mission…Christ painstakingly invested himself in twelve hand-chosen people. He selected three of them for more intimate relationships.
>
> "The book of Acts shows us the powerful results. This handful of apprentices lit the spark that caused the Gospel to spread like a flash-fire in the first century. As Christians today, we can trace our roots to these carefully trained and Holy Spirit empowered men."[5]

The realities of life today do not permit the kind of extended time Jesus was able to spend with his disciples. The principle still holds, however. So how does a youth minister spend more time developing the students with leadership potential without neglecting the others he or she has been hired to shepherd?

There is a way, and as you've already seen, it isn't new. Its effectiveness has been proven over millennia. Although temporarily shelved in favor of "more efficient" means of informational mass transfer via lectures and media, it is once again making a resurgence. We are learning, as perhaps every generation must, that efficiency does not always equal effectiveness. Mentoring provides balance, significance, and emotional fuel in a high-tech, high-demand, fast-paced world.

Chuck Colson said, "As I look back on my Christian life, I realize

> *How does a youth minister spend more time with a few and without neglecting the others he or she has been hired to shepherd?*

that my mentoring experiences were absolutely indispensable. Without any question, my experience with Jesus Christ was real, but where it would have led me apart from the patient tutoring and unconditional love of this small group of men is anyone's guess."[6]

Emerging Young Leaders: One Approach to Mentoring

Emerging Young Leaders (EYL) is a nonprofit ministry organization whose vision is to see emerging young leaders in every nation equipped to serve with integrity and excellence in strategic leadership roles. Our mission is to provide resources for mentoring and to train the world's emerging young leaders for significant service and the development of others.

Why are we so concerned about developing leadership? There are two simple reasons. The first is its crucial importance to the Body of Christ. Bobb Biehl, in his excellent book *Mentoring,* says:

> If you took the senior pastor of the largest church in America today and put him in another city, in five years you'd have another major church. If you took a weak pastor and put him at the largest church in the country, in five years you'd have a shell. Every organizational unit is a direct reflection of the leadership it has been given. Leadership is critical to the strength and health of the Christian body.[7]

The second reason for our emphasis on leadership is the lack of it in today's younger generations. These are the people who must fill the shoes of the visionary leaders of the 1940s and 50s—the men and women who were responsible for founding a majority of the world's mission organizations and parachurch ministries. It's one thing to complete a ministry track in a Bible school or Christian liberal arts college and be prepared to "minister." It's quite another to have the passion and skills required to effectively motivate and lead a group of people. From all sectors of our global society—secular as well as Christian—people are expressing alarm over the need for young leadership.

If we're going to fill the leadership vacuum that exists in the world today, we need to build young people who have passion, not just young people who have interests. At Emerging Young Leaders, we emphasize that mentoring should be purposeful and should have a specific goal. We are not content to simply provide a hand-holding experience for students who are loaded with potential but aren't being challenged to develop it. We're calling students to become the kind of world-changers God designed them to be.

Does that mean we exclude "average" or "below average" achievers from the mentoring process? By no means! We encourage mentoring for every willing young person. Through the mentoring process, those with leadership abilities and desires can be identified and offered advanced leadership training. But all protégés will benefit from the blend of character and competency attributes upon which our mentoring model is built.

Our Unique Mentoring Model

Emerging Young Leaders promotes a one-to-three mentoring model that encourages one mentor for three young people of the same gender. There are several compelling reasons and benefits.

Volunteer mentors need protection from suspicion. An adult meeting regularly with an unrelated single young person is a common target for accusations these days. The potential for sexual misconduct has become a very sensitive issue.

> *The potential for sexual misconduct has become a very sensitive issue.*

Also, the typical one-to-one model makes it much more difficult to extend the mentoring opportunity to all willing students. The difficulty is rarely a lack of willing protégés; it's almost always a lack of willing mentors. Our one-to-three model enables three times as many young people to enter into mentoring relationships. We don't recommend protégé groups larger than three because of the change that occurs in the group's dynamics. When there are four or five young people, they relate more to each other than to the mentor.

Mentors with three young people have three times the potential for real success stories—a clear indication that their time is well spent. This kind of reward is powerful in keeping them involved and growing in commitment.

Mentors with multiple young people face reduced risk of an unacceptable mismatch. There is a natural cushion provided by the interaction of the students themselves that softens an otherwise potentially uncomfortable chemistry between a mentor and a single protégé.

Our mentoring model makes use of a mentor's guide, *Successful Youth Mentoring,* strategically designed for either parents or adult volunteers to use with teenage protégés. To successfully develop servant leadership in young people, we address two categories of issues: those that are character-based and those that are competency- or skill-based. Character is like direction, and competency is like speed. Competency encompasses skills that can be used to achieve a goal. Character determines what the goal should be in the first place.

Integrity, personal discipline, concern for others, positive attitude, moral values, commitment to excellence, and healthy ego strength are a few examples of character issues. Competency issues include organizational skills, time management, communication skills, planning, attention to detail, and others.

> Competency *encompasses skills that can be used to achieve a goal.* Character *determines what the goal should be in the first place.*

To keep a consistently healthy ratio of character and competency qualities in the mentoring curriculum, EYL offers a repeating structure. Each six-week unit is built on six characteristics of a servant leader. Even though only one of them is specifically called "character," most of them are character-based. They are courage, compassion, competency, character, conviction, and commitment.

Every mentoring session is formatted identically and includes six major components:

● For Mentors Only—a brief section that provides the mentor with the objectives and background material for the session.

● Introducing the Concept—several detailed options such as activities, stories, and questions to help mentors get into the topic with their young people.

● The Truth Statement—a brief, memorable statement that embodies the heart and soul of the session; something they can easily hang on to.

● The Lesson—several options that get into the depth of the subject and provide practical help in both character and competency issues.

● Ancient Wisdom—the scriptural principle, including a memory verse.

● The Closing—a short recap of the highlights. It sometimes includes an assignment that can be done individually or together during the following week.

EYL's Mentoring Covenant

The mentoring covenant helps clarify expectations and define the commitment that is expected on both sides of the relationship.

● *Mentors* commit to a modeling and teaching relationship in which they challenge and encourage young people to become servant leaders.

● *Protégés* commit to a relationship of learning and accountability in which they are challenged and encouraged to become servant leaders.

The Need for Volunteers

Adult volunteers always sound like a good idea until you try to recruit. It can be like pulling teeth, and for good reasons.

They don't want to be baby-sitters or policemen.

They feel unprepared to "run the show" from the stage.

They fear being ridiculed because they aren't in touch with the latest fads, expressions, and devices used by teens to let the rest of the world know it doesn't belong in their domain.

They don't feel confident with larger groups.

But despite the misgivings, many adults are willing to volunteer if they can make a measurable difference in the lives of even a few kids.

Mentors need a tool to give them confidence.

What mentors bring to the table from their own experience is a key component.

Two Strong Reasons for Using a Mentoring Guide

Simply asking adult volunteers to mentor young people is not enough. Most adults will initially feel inadequate for the role. They feel unprepared to use their knowledge and experience in a way that won't bore teenagers to death. They need a tool to give them confidence so they can perform with excellence. (For more on recruiting and training mentors, see pages 98-99.)

This is the first of two major reasons why EYL has developed a mentoring guide that goes far beyond simple tips and techniques. *Successful Youth Mentoring* provides actual mentoring sessions, complete with multiple options that can be tailored to the needs of the individual. This user-friendly curriculum draws adult volunteers who wouldn't otherwise consider mentoring young people.

The second reason we designed the curriculum is to provide assurance that there would be significant content and value in each mentoring encounter. We understand that the relationship that develops between mentor and protégés is vitally important, and that what mentors bring to the table from their own experience is a key component. But we also know that all mentors are not equal, and that some have less experience and depth of knowledge than others.

Others may have the experience and knowledge but need a structure that will bring it out. *Successful Youth Mentoring* helps level the playing field and elevates all mentors to a higher level. It provides framework, content, questions, ideas, options, instruction—everything needed to take an average adult volunteer and make him or her an above-average mentor.

Our definition of mentoring: a teaching and learning relationship in which one person invests in others as a steward of time and resources.

> *Mentoring is a teaching and learning relationship in which one person invests in others as a steward of time and resources.*

> *Don't underestimate the value of meeting regularly at the same time and place.*

Location and Time Considerations

Encourage mentors to schedule meetings in a comfortable and safe place. Mentoring sessions can occur almost anywhere—indoors, outdoors, at home, at church, in a restaurant, at a park, in the library. Don't underestimate the value of meeting regularly at the same time and place. The more protégés you have and the younger they are, the more important this will be. There will be enough natural obstacles to perfect attendance; don't add more by the confusion that results from odd or inconsistent times and places.

The content of a particular session may dictate a location with a VCR or a computer. Or it may suggest visiting a museum, a factory, a sporting event, a mall, or another location that will illustrate a point. Some sessions might be of a sensitive nature and would be best conducted in a more private setting.

Freedom and creativity are important in a good mentoring relationship, but they do require some precautions. For instance, when a mentor chooses to take a field trip as part of a session, have the mentor and the protégés try to meet at the normal time and place and go together from there so that no one is confused about the meeting place. When that isn't possible, be sure to overcommunicate. Telephone reminders the day before are not overkill.

Have mentors determine up front how long and how frequent their meetings will be. We have designed our sessions to take an hour or less each, and to occur weekly in six-week units with a short break between units. The six-week unit approach removes two critical concerns:

● It allows the mentor to make a short initial commitment. With a positive initial experience, mentors often continue for years.

● It allows for an easier change in mentor/protégé match-up in those rare instances where the chemistry just doesn't work.

Recruiting and Training Mentors

Any effective mentoring program requires several adult mentors. Mobilizing adults is a two-stage process. First they must be recruited, and then they must be trained. Both jobs are easier when a quality curriculum is available.

Every great tool has an attraction of its own.

Recruiting

The fact that adults usually require a tool that gives them confidence before they will enlist as volunteers has already been mentioned. Furthermore, every great tool has an attraction of its own. Some adults have purchased *Successful Youth Mentoring* without anyone in mind to mentor; they recognized its value and felt they had to make use of it somehow.

A source of volunteer mentors that should not be overlooked is the parents of young people in your group. *Successful Youth Mentoring* was designed to comfortably accommodate fathers and mothers who want to mentor their sons and daughters. It's still a good idea to mentor groups of three. The son or daughter can invite friends (inside or outside the church) who would enjoy and benefit from the mentoring experience. Young people from single-parent homes are a great choice for joining a father-son or mother-daughter group.

The most powerful recruiting tool is the training workshop, described in the next few paragraphs.

Training

Training mentors is easier when you use a curriculum like *Successful Youth Mentoring* that trains them as they go. With material that guides them through each mentoring session, mentors don't have to have a university degree in mentoring. They can start with confidence and improve as they go. As with many new challenges, the most valuable training often happens on the job.

While we believe strongly in on-the-job training for mentors, we also offer mentor training through workshops, seminars, Sunday school classes, retreats, and other forums. One of the most effective methods is to host a half-day training workshop. This also will be your strongest recruitment vehicle.

The most valuable training often happens on the job.

You may want to make appeals for mentors in Sunday morning services, as well as in any other forum. Highlight the value of mentoring, and offer the workshop for everyone who has interest. It's usually best to avoid requesting or accepting a commitment to become a mentor prior to the initial workshop.

The half-day workshop we've prepared for churches consists of a trained volunteer facilitator with video support. It includes the following four sessions:

- Introduction to Mentor Training
- Mentoring: How to Speak Into Someone's Life
- Dealing With Difficulties in Mentoring
- Meeting With Your Protégés

The workshop is inspirational and instructional; most who attend are ready to sign up before they leave. This jump-starts a mentoring program and creates a powerful sense of momentum. It also forms the basis for fellowship among mentors, which is an important element in their continued growth and success.

One downside of making a general appeal is the possibility of being approached by people who are unfit for the role. It may require some delicate diplomacy to decline their offers of involvement. The requirement to attend the workshop will weed some of them out. Others will attend and decide not to pursue mentoring based on the commitment. Still others may need to be at least temporarily set aside because of their inability to meet minimum standards.

A different approach is to preselect people in whom you have confidence and specifically invite them to the workshop. Regardless of how you handle the invitation process, you'll want to develop screening criteria for prospective mentors. Failure to take appropriate safety precautions could result in an unfortunate or tragic surprise.

Just as churches vary in size and location, so do their needs in screening prospective mentors. At the very least, you should use the same criteria you use to evaluate potential volunteer staff for youth ministry. These typically include an application, references, membership in the church, and a background check.

Matching Mentors and Protégés

Mentoring relationships in which young people have a voice in choosing their mentors enjoy a longer life span, on average, than those in which people are arbitrarily assigned. Some students aren't particularly concerned with the matchup; others are very concerned. We recommend allowing at least the latter group to indicate their preferences from among available mentors. They must understand that their preferences may not be available but that their choices will be accommodated if possible. It's helpful to point out that some adults who are better known or more popular with students may not always be the best mentors.

Chemistry and personality match between mentors and young people are important in inverse relationship to the motivation and maturity of the teenager. If you hope to keep an immature, unmotivated teenager in a mentoring relationship, the chemistry must be strong. If the match isn't a perfect fit, though, most students will be satisfied with a brief explanation. A mentor who is not a natural match offers a broadened perspective—like a cross-cultural experience.

The Care and Feeding of Mentors

Recognition and appreciation are rarely overused. An anecdote about the leadership of Napoleon helps us visualize this important truth. In an effort to strengthen the loyalty of his troops, he routinely visited his army's field locations.

Prior to making an appearance, Napoleon would consult with the regiment's commanding officer and get the name of a soldier who had served with distinction but had not been adequately recognized. He would then request background information about the man and commit the highlights to memory. After agreeing on a subtle cue by which the commander could identify the man to Napoleon, the regiment review would begin.

When Napoleon came to the soldier, he would single him out by name and hold a brief conversation with him in which he talked about the man's family, his service on the field of battle, etc. The results were dramatic. All the others could be heard whispering to each other, "Do you see that? He cares. He knows about us. He knows we have served."[8]

> *"He knows we have served."*

Napoleon's practice was a means to an end. We aren't advocating manipulation, but there is within each of us a deep desire to have our service recognized and appreciated. God knows we have served, but our service is more joyful—and usually more excellent—if we believe someone else knows, too.

One means of providing support for volunteer mentors is by beginning a Sunday school class or an adult Bible fellowship specifically for them. It may begin as a six-week unit followed by an evaluation to determine its continuation. There should be time for prayer support, sharing creative ideas, and clarification of difficult issues. This creates a system of mutual support and strong commitment.

The nurturing and support of any volunteer is vitally important to his or her success. The youth director should make the commitment to call each mentor every month. The call usually doesn't need to last long. It can flow naturally from some relationship-building small talk to a few questions that will give some valuable insight and help keep the mentor on track and motivated.

Be sure to let mentors know right away that you're making routine calls to see how the mentors are doing. Don't let them wonder whether you've gotten some bad feedback on them and are just waiting to drop a bomb. Let them know that you appreciate their dedication and that you're excited about the process. Assure them that the real impact of their efforts may not surface for years. Then ask a few questions such as "How do you feel about the process?" "Is it comfortable? If not, do you see it becoming more comfortable with a little more time?" "What could make it better?" and "What can I do to help you in the process?"

You should have a list of the names and numbers for all the groups. This will help you ask specific questions: "How is John doing? Do you have a feel for what his interests are? Does he seem to click well with the others in your protégé group? Are there some things you're praying for him about?" (Be careful not to violate confidentiality. We'll talk more about that later; see pages 101-102.)

Although it will be a chore for some personality types to call the volunteer mentors on a monthly basis, the benefits are more than worth the effort. Your regular contact will

- demonstrate the importance of mentoring in your priorities,
- validate the mentor as a ministry partner,
- allow you to gain deeper insight into some of your students,
- encourage accountability and quality effort from mentors,
- help clarify questions the mentors otherwise might not raise,
- enable mentors to share positive experiences from the lives of teenagers,
- raise warning flags if a relationship needs changing or adjustment, and
- allow natural networking to additional potential mentors.

The real impact of their efforts may not surface for years.

The Importance of Confidentiality

Here's an important word of caution that is critical for mentors, especially if they meet together in a setting where they're likely to know protégés other than their own: It's very important that mentors maintain a high degree of confidentiality regarding their protégés. Questions and discussions will naturally arise in a mentor group setting, some of which could contain uncomplimentary information about young people. Mentors must make two commitments at the very outset and periodically reaffirm them:

- They will not identify the young person who makes a statement or exhibits behavior that comes under discussion by the class or group of mentors.
- In cases where a slip is made or it is obvious who the young person is, other mentors will not pass the information along or make any mention of it to the young person or anyone else—even as a light-hearted jest.

Breaking confidentiality undermines the integrity of the mentor in the eyes of the protégé.

Many people can keep confidences they know are important. But many of those same people would mistakenly identify some information as unimportant. They might find it difficult, for instance, upon hearing some humorous or positive incident regarding a teenager they know well, to keep it to themselves. The temptation can be very strong to mention it, even as a compliment.

The problem is that the young people immediately know the source of the information and quickly discern that anything they say or do in the presence of their mentor might become public. This damages trust in the relationship and undermines the integrity of the mentor in the eyes of the protégé.

Mentors with multiple protégés meeting together must encourage their young people to adopt the same commitment toward each other. Although mentoring is neither purely counseling nor accountability, there are aspects of both involved. For the mentoring relationship to work at an optimal level, a sense of trust and mutual protection needs to be established early.

Be very careful about compromising confidentiality in the quest for prayer support. Some young people may be experiencing difficulties that require diligent prayer from many people. An issue that is not already public knowledge must not become public knowledge as a result of a mentor's efforts to solicit prayer support. Sincere people of prayer are frequently called upon to do spiritual battle without knowing all the details or the identity of their subject. God knows and will reward both their efforts and their restraint in not requiring all the gory details.

There are some kinds of information that must be passed on to the appropriate people in a responsible way. Issues of abuse or behavior that could be seriously damaging to someone require something beyond confidentiality. Within a church setting, a pastor should determine what steps need to be taken. Once the mentor has gone to a pastor with the issue, the mentor must return to the confidentiality mode.

Evaluating Success

Most management consultants place high value on measurements. Quantifying results is an important element in determining whether you have achieved your objectives. Gauging the success of a mentoring relationship, however, is not always easy. Defining expectations at the outset is a good start.

Successful mentoring often occurs without immediately dramatic results.

Both sides of the relationship need to realize that successful mentoring can, and often does, occur without dramatic results. The same might be said of daily Bible reading and prayer. At the very least, we know the discipline is good for us. We can discern growth, but it's hard to see on a daily basis. Someone who journals could look back at entries a year earlier and see evidence of the maturing process. It's like measuring the growth of a tree. Just watching it from day to day, you might think it's not growing at all, but a glance at the rings shows a steady annual increase.

Since life never gives us the opportunity to go down two paths simultaneously, we can never be certain of what would have happened if we had chosen a different track. Past experience leads us to believe, however, that there are some things we wouldn't have learned if we had not exposed ourselves to learning opportunities. Students should be able to look back on a year of mentoring and see character qualities and leadership skills they have developed.

A concept that is equally valid, but even more difficult to grasp, is the number of problems or even disasters we have avoided by virtue of the path we have chosen. We may not think often in these terms, but imagine the physical, spiritual, and emotional damage we avoid by simply obeying God's design for expressing our sexuality. A good accountability relationship provides some of this preventive benefit. Young people should be able to look back on a year of mentoring and, without too much difficulty, imagine some of the mistakes they might have made in the absence of their mentoring experiences.

Some individuals need considerable feedback in order to see evidence of their own growth.

Keep in mind, however, that some individuals need considerable feedback in order to see evidence of their own growth. I recently asked a young man in my Sunday school class whether he could see growth in his life over the last year or two. He thought for a moment and said, "No, I don't think so."

I don't know him well, so I didn't press the issue in front of the class, but later I asked someone who does know him well. He couldn't believe the student's response. "Ask his parents," he said. "Ask anybody who knows him. There's been tremendous change and growth in his life!"

Some people—even some who behave very badly—have unrealistically high standards for themselves. Others may never have felt unconditionally loved and accepted and feel that they can never measure up. No matter how much growth there might be, they have a perfectionist attitude that doesn't allow them to recognize improvement. The result for some is hostility and rebellion. For others it may be resignation or apathy. Positive, honest feedback from a mentor regarding even slight growth in a young person can be a huge encouragement—one that unlocks the door to much greater and faster growth.

> *Young people should express appreciation for their mentors' efforts.*

Encourage mentors to keep at least simple journals of their own journeys. They should also encourage teenagers to do the same. One of the most valuable uses of a journal is to note small, private victories. It's the succession of these small, private victories that helps us build courage and faith, spurring us on to greater successes and public victories.

Both mentors and protégés must accept by faith that growth is virtually inherent in a mentoring relationship, even if it's slow and subtle. Young people should be instructed (by someone other than their mentors!) that it's important to express appreciation for their mentors' efforts. Feedback from teenagers is essential in letting mentors know they're accomplishing something worthwhile.

Mentoring
Available to all young people

Identification
Leaders are identified

Training
Advanced leadership-training experiences for those who qualify

Multiplication
Protégés, after being mentored and trained, reproduce themselves in ever-increasing numbers

Emerging Young Leaders offers leadership development training experiences that are supplemental to the mentoring program. The complete process resembles an hourglass in design. (See the illustration in the margin.) All young people are encouraged to enter the mentoring program through their local church or parachurch organization. This is the large top of the hourglass. Through the process of mentoring, students with leadership potential are identified and encouraged to participate in leadership-training experiences. The training is the narrower midsection of the hourglass. The end result is that trained leaders will multiply themselves many times over. This is the large base of the hourglass.

EYL has developed specific guidelines for what a trained emerging young leader should look like. The following standards of achievement and excellence could be adapted to your own program.

Standards of Achievement
- Character — Involvement in an accountability relationship
- Courage — A leadership role
- Compassion — Cross-cultural and community service experience
- Competency — Thirty hours of EYL leadership-development training

- Conviction
- Commitment

Evangelism/discipleship training and involvement

Has been mentored for a minimum of one year

Standard of Excellence

- Character
- Courage
- Compassion
- Competency
- Conviction

- Commitment

Continued accountability

Ongoing leadership role

International service experience

Twenty additional hours of training

Has shared his or her faith and is involved in discipling someone

Has a minimum of one additional year of leadership mentoring

It may be that your program will develop less emphasis on leadership training. You may desire a different outcome. Whatever your goal for the end product is, try to state it in terms of involvement and process—not awards or arrivals. Only one person can win a race in which others are involved, but everyone can participate. More important, everyone can win his or her own race.

> *Everyone can win his or her own race.*

Develop some measurable, attainable goals for your mentoring program so that you can enjoy the sweet fulfillment of progress and accomplishment.

Involvement in evangelism and discipleship is a high priority in the development of the next generation of leaders. EYL's vision and mission are stated in secular language to allow us access into countries that aren't open to traditional missionary organizations. Our final goal, however, is the multiplication of leaders who are committed disciples of Jesus Christ. They will not only serve with excellence in their chosen careers, but will be committed to multiplying their personal impact through personal evangelism and discipleship.

We believe that a mentoring program for your young people should be at the top of your ministry priority list. There is no church too small or too large to implement one. It doesn't require paid staff to supervise, nor is mentoring a passing fad whose relevance will soon be outdated. It is simply an ancient tried-and-true method we have neglected. You can do it. You should do it. We are ready to help you do it.

Endnotes

1. Tony Campolo, *Who Switched the Price Tags?* (Waco, TX: Word Books, 1986), 69-72.

2. Glenn Van Ekeren, *Speaker's Sourcebook II* (Englewood Cliffs, NJ: Prentice-Hall, Inc., 1994), 60.

3. Van Ekeren, *Speaker's Sourcebook II*, 57.

4. Van Ekeren, *Speaker's Sourcebook II*, 58.

5. Bill LeTourneau, "Emerging Young Leaders: Mentoring Tomorrow's Leaders Today," a brochure by EYL.

6. Ted W. Engstrom with Norman B. Rohrer, *The Fine Art of Mentoring* (Newburgh, IN: Trinity Press, 1994), 40.

7. Bobb Biehl, *Mentoring* (Nashville, TN: Broadman & Holman Publishers, 1996), 144.

8. Joe Taylor Ford, *Sourcebook of Wit & Wisdom,* (Canton, OH: Communication Resources, Inc., 1996), 135.

Additional Resources for Mentoring

Biehl, Bobb. *Mentoring.* Nashville, TN: Broadman & Holman Publishers, 1996.

Clinton, J. Robert and Paul D. Stanley. *Connecting.* Colorado Springs, CO: NavPress, 1992.

Downer, Phil with Chip MacGregor. *Eternal Impact.* Eugene, OR: Harvest House Publishers Inc., 1997.

Elmore, Tim. *Mentoring.* Indianapolis, IN: Wesleyan Publishing House and Kingdom Publishing House, 1995.

Elmore, Tim. *The Greatest Mentors in the Bible.* Denver, CO: Kingdom Publishing House, 1996.

Engstrom, Ted W. with Norman B. Rohrer. *The Fine Art of Mentoring.* Newburgh, IN: Trinity Press, 1994.

Getz, Gene A. *Building up One Another.* Wheaton, IL: Victor Books, 1997.

Hendricks, Howard G. and William D. Hendricks. *As Iron Sharpens Iron.* Chicago, IL: Moody Press, 1995.

Kingdom Building Ministries. *It's My Turn.* Denver, CO: Kingdom Publishing House, 1996.

Otto, Donna. *The Gentle Art of Mentoring.* Eugene, OR: Harvest House Publishers Inc., 1997.

Stout, William T. and Becker, James K. *The Good Shepherd Program: Tools to Protect Your Church by Preventing Child Abuse.* Fort Collins, CO: NEXUS Solutions, 1996.

Group Publishing, Inc.
Attention: Product Development
P.O. Box 481
Loveland, CO 80539
Fax: (970) 669-1994

Evaluation for INTENSIVE CARING:
PRACTICAL WAYS TO MENTOR YOUTH

Please help Group Publishing, Inc., continue to provide innovative and useful resources for ministry. Please take a moment to fill out this evaluation and mail or fax it to us. Thanks!

● ● ●

1. As a whole, this book has been (circle one)

not very helpful   very helpful

1   2   3   4   5   6   7   8   9   10

2. The best things about this book:

3. Ways this book could be improved:

4. Things I will change because of this book:

5. Other books I'd like to see Group publish in the future:

6. Would you be interested in field-testing future Group products and giving us your feedback? If so, please fill in the information below:

Name _____

Street Address _____

City _____ State _____ Zip _____

Phone Number _____ Date _____

Exciting Resources for Your Adult Ministry

Sermon-Booster Dramas

Tim Kurth

Now you can deliver powerful messages in fresh, new ways. Set up your message with memorable, easy-to-produce dramas—each just 3 minutes or less! These 25 low-prep dramas hit hot topics ranging from burnout...ethics...parenting...stress...to work...career issues and more! Your listeners will be on the edge of their seats!

ISBN 0-7644-2016-X

Fun Friend-Making Activities for Adult Groups

Karen Dockrey

More than 50 relational programming ideas help even shy adults talk with others at church! You'll find low-risk Icebreakers to get adults introduced and talking...Camaraderie-Builders that help adults connect and start talking about what's really happening in their lives...and Friend-Makers to cement friendships with authentic sharing and accountability.

ISBN 0-7644-2011-9

Bore No More (For Every Pastor, Speaker, Teacher)

Mike & Amy Nappa

This is a must-have for pastors, college/career speakers, and others who address groups! Because rather than just provide illustrations to entertain audiences, the authors show readers how to involve audiences in the learning process. The 70 sermon ideas presented are based on New Testament passages, but the principles apply to all passages.

ISBN 1-55945-266-8

Young Adult Faith-Launchers

These 18 in-depth Bible studies are perfect for young adults who want to strengthen their faith and deepen their relationships. They will explore real-world issues...ask the tough questions...and along the way turn casual relationships into supportive, caring friendships. Quick prep and high involvement make these the ideal studies for peer-led Bible studies, small groups, and classes.

ISBN 0-7644-2037-2

Order today from your local Christian bookstore, or write: Group Publishing, P.O. Box 485, Loveland, CO 80539.

Bible Study Series

Give Your Teenagers a Solid Faith Foundation That Lasts a Lifetime!

Here are the *essentials* of the Christian life—core values teenagers *must* believe to make good decisions now...and build an *unshakable* lifelong faith. Developed by youth workers like you...field-tested with *real* youth groups in *real* churches...here's the meat your kids *must* have to grow spiritually—presented in a fun, involving way!

Each 4-session **Core Belief Bible Study Series** book lets you easily...
- Lead deep, compelling, *relevant* discussions your kids won't want to miss...
- Involve teenagers in exploring life-changing truths...
- Help kids create healthy relationships with each other—and you!

Plus you'll make an *eternal difference* in the lives of your kids as you give them a solid faith foundation that stands firm on God's Word.

Here are the Core Belief Bible Study Series titles already available...

Senior High Studies

Why **Authority** Matters	0-7644-0892-5
Why **Being a Christian** Matters	0-7644-0883-6
Why **Creation** Matters	0-7644-0880-1
Why **Forgiveness** Matters	0-7644-0887-9
Why **God** Matters	0-7644-0874-7
Why **God's Justice** Matters	0-7644-0886-0
Why **Jesus Christ** Matters	0-7644-0875-5
Why **Love** Matters	0-7644-0889-5
Why **Our Families** Matter	0-7644-0894-1
Why **Personal Character** Matters	0-7644-0885-2
Why **Prayer** Matters	0-7644-0893-3
Why **Relationships** Matter	0-7644-0896-8
Why **Serving Others** Matters	0-7644-0895-X
Why **Spiritual Growth** Matters	0-7644-0884-4
Why **Suffering** Matters	0-7644-0879-8
Why **the Bible** Matters	0-7644-0882-8
Why **the Church** Matters	0-7644-0890-9
Why **the Holy Spirit** Matters	0-7644-0876-3
Why **the Last Days** Matter	0-7644-0888-7
Why **the Spiritual Realm** Matters	0-7644-0881-X
Why **Worship** Matters	0-7644-0891-7

Junior High/Middle School Studies

The Truth About **Authority**	0-7644-0868-2
The Truth About **Being a Christian**	0-7644-0859-3
The Truth About **Creation**	0-7644-0856-9
The Truth About **Developing Character**	0-7644-0861-5
The Truth About **God**	0-7644-0850-X
The Truth About **God's Justice**	0-7644-0862-3
The Truth About **Jesus Christ**	0-7644-0851-8
The Truth About **Love**	0-7644-0865-8
The Truth About **Our Families**	0-7644-0870-4
The Truth About **Prayer**	0-7644-0869-0
The Truth About **Relationships**	0-7644-0872-0
The Truth About **Serving Others**	0-7644-0871-2
The Truth About **Sin and Forgiveness**	0-7644-0863-1
The Truth About **Spiritual Growth**	0-7644-0860-7
The Truth About **Suffering**	0-7644-0855-0
The Truth About **the Bible**	0-7644-0858-5
The Truth About **the Church**	0-7644-0899-2
The Truth About **the Holy Spirit**	0-7644-0852-6
The Truth About **the Last Days**	0-7644-0864-X
The Truth About **the Spiritual Realm**	0-7644-0857-7
The Truth About **Worship**	0-7644-0867-4

BRING THE BIBLE TO LIFE FOR YOUR 1ST- THROUGH 6TH-GRADERS... WITH GROUP'S HANDS-ON BIBLE CURRICULUM™

Energize your kids with Active Learning!

Group's **Hands-On Bible Curriculum**™ will help you teach the Bible in a radical new way. It's based on Active Learning—the same teaching method Jesus used.

In each lesson, students will participate in exciting and memorable learning experiences using fascinating gadgets and gizmos you've not seen with any other curriculum. Your elementary students will discover biblical truths and <u>remember</u> what they learn because they're <u>doing</u> instead of just listening.

You'll save time and money, too!

While students are learning more, you'll be working less—simply follow the quick and easy instructions in the **Teacher Guide**. You'll get tons of material for an energy-packed 35- to 60-minute lesson. And, if you have extra time, there's an arsenal of Bonus Ideas and Time Stuffers to keep kids occupied—and learning! Plus, you'll SAVE BIG over other curriculum programs that require you to buy expensive separate student books—all student handouts in Group's **Hands-On Bible Curriculum** are photocopiable!

In addition to the easy-to-use **Teacher Guide**, you'll get all the essential teaching materials you need in a ready-to-use **Learning Lab**®. No more running from store to store hunting for lesson materials—all the active-learning tools you need to teach 13 exciting Bible lessons to any size class are provided for you in the **Learning Lab**.

Challenging topics each quarter keep your kids coming back!

Group's **Hands-On Bible Curriculum** covers topics that matter to your kids and teaches them the Bible with integrity. Switching topics every month keeps your 1st- through 6th-graders enthused and coming back for more. The full two-year program will help your kids...

> •make God-pleasing decisions,
> •recognize their God-given potential, and
> •seek to grow as Christians.

Take the boredom out of Sunday school, children's church, and midweek meetings for your elementary students. Make your job easier and more rewarding with no-fail lessons that are ready in a flash. Order Group's **Hands-On Bible Curriculum** for your 1st- through 6th-graders today.

Hands-On Bible Curriculum is also available for Toddlers & 2s, Preschool, and Pre-K and K!

Order today from your local Christian bookstore, or write: Group Publishing, P.O. Box 485, Loveland, CO 80539.